MW01624834

All too often, Christians who are sinners themselves become judge, jury, and jailer of each other. In his newest release, *Why We Eat Our Own*, author and pastor Michael Cheshire boldly explores some unsavory questions:

-Why does the world often do a better job of forgiving their fallen than the Church?
-Is the decline in Christianity due to the world, or have we just become horrible to each other and the world noted it?

Dedication

To my children:
Chloe, Titus, and Silas
May you be bold, kind and passionate in all you say and do, and may you always follow Jesus, even when it goes against Christianity.

Thanks to my Gangsta Nation of friends:

Amy: my wife, my girlfriend, and my love. She is the jam in my jelly roll.
Cortland: who looks 12 but leads like a Roman general
Emily: who runs my life, knows all my pass codes, decides where I go, and find my lost luggage.
Sterling: who gave me classes on how to be Black...
And now I am.....
Nicole S: my psychologist - After this book ,we have a whole new boatload of things to deal with, so we can forget about the dad issues for a while
Andrew S: graphic artist extraordinaire - The book looks great, now let's get working on photoshopping abs on all my pictures
Jmac: whose choice of beer, cigars and leaders is unparalleled
Tiny: who handles all the money from all our businesses; she is my favorite
Adam: the man that can fix anything.... except a nasty break dance habit
Brian: who loves the Chicago Bears and Norte Dame, thus he is well acquainted with sorrow
Melissa: who is the glue for us all - the force is strong in this one
Andrew Z: who proves all the dumb rumors about homeschoolers are completely true
Ellie: she's new but fierce
Cindi: the happiest person I know
Jenn Clark: if you like my writing it's because of her;
if you hate my writing it's because of her
Daphne: whose accent could make even insults sound great
Jim: who believes Bigfoot is real yet swears he doesn't
hit the Mary Jane
Steve: who believes the best in his friends
Our Elders- Michelle, Jay, Patsy, Coleen and Terry. - The Wise Ones

And, of course, thanks to the many Journey peeps who I left out and who will remind me later to my great shame.

If you think your education
will open doors for you to matter,
you need more education.

#WhyWeEatOurOwn

Table of Contents

A few caveats and disclaimers:

Let's get on the same page . . .
or Kindle or Nook or iPhone or Ipad or
whatever you're reading this on.

I use the word "church" often in this book.
Please know that I do understand that people "are" the Church and not a building.
It's just easier to use it in the context of communities of worship. Okay? No emails on this one.

I didn't stop every other sentence and quote Scripture. If you have even a basic understanding of Scripture, you will see the principles clearly.

I repeat some of the same themes at times.
Some things just need to be hammered home.

I started this publishing company with my best friends. We are still learning. You may see some mistakes. Let's just say we left them there so you can see we are not perfect. Yea. Yea. Thats why they are there.

Even though I'm very blunt at times,
please know that
I love the Church.
Completely. Always have, always will.

May you find the peace you need.
And may you have the courage to go get it, even if it's on the other side of war.
-Michael Cheshire

Forward

JONATHAN BROZOZOG

As a fifth-generation pastor, I'm all too familiar with church culture. I've lived with deacons, bishops, apostles, and church mothers. I have heard shofars blown, seen praise dancers twirl, and have dusted my fair share of silk plants. I've also seen the uglier side of church; I've witnessed how badly people were treated when they fell.

I met with a fellow pastor at Waffle House before heading to my first Grace Initiative Round Table. Over breakfast, I shared a frustration I had with a leader in my church who was struggling with a sin issue. For those of you who don't know, "struggling" is Christianese for "still doing it." Though the leader repented and desired change, I found myself wrestling with how to handle the matter. Do I sideline him for a season or permanently remove him from his position for the greater good and protection of the church? I am a pastor after all. At the end of the day, part of my job is to protect the church. Right?

At the Round Table, Pastor Ted Haggard, his wife, Gayle, and Michael Cheshire led great discussions shedding light on genuine love and the truth of New Testament grace. I felt as if I was being shown a treasure I had all along but was hidden in plain sight.

"Could we be wrong?" I thought as I left. "Could we be wrong about how we approach redemption and grace? Why have I been taught so much about church discipline and correction and taught so little about grace, love, and restoration?"

Why does the Church eat its own? How can the world have better examples of restoring people than the Church? I left the Round Table with a new perspective on grace that was actually worth something; but I realized, that back at my church, I was building something with a serious flaw. The model of grace I had been taught added no value to people's lives. Today's Church shows a grace that is distant, unforgiving and void of love. It is what I call Worthless Grace.

What if we did something different? What if we started to change how we tended to our wounded, regardless of the situation, regardless of the sin? Imagine a church where we focused more on the people and less on their issues. What if we preached grace and repentance with a Christ-like mind and Christ-like love? Grace like that could change the world! And what the Church needs now are more men and women who have the courage to defend New Testament grace at all cost. Trust me when I tell you, it will cost you.

Why this book is so important:

The one thing I learned about falling is that no one chooses where they fall. They just fall. It's not as if when walking down the street I tell myself, "Hey, when I get to the corner, I'm going to fall." It just happens. When people fall (as we all do), the Church needs to be in a position to show people love. What Michael has done with this book is shine a light on a hidden truth; when it comes to showing grace, the Church is an epic failure.

The Church has to become better at showing grace because the world needs it. The Church needs it.

This book will challenge your thinking about grace and redemption. Michael takes a brass knuckle approach at defending New Testament grace and the Grace Initiative.

One of the points Michael emphasizes in *Why We Eat Our Own* is that it takes courage to live out

New Testament grace.

New Testament grace is based on love, and authentic love is manifested in giving. This type of grace will require you to give something of yourself. In this book, Michael challenges you to do some self-examination and ask yourself, "What am I willing to lose to ensure people receive God's best for their lives?" This book has the potential to radically change how the Church tends to its wounded.

So sit back and hold on as you are about to be challenged and stretched. You may even laugh until you cry, but it is my hope that you realize you may have been wrong about grace and redemption all along.

People who speak with
conviction are rarely heard,
but they are ALWAYS felt.
They alone will change the world.
#WhyWeEatOurOwn

#why we eat our own 1

Why This Book?

"I can't believe the news today,
Oh, I can't close my eyes and make it go away,
How long, how long must we sing this song?
How long? How long?
'Cause tonight we can be as one, tonight"
U2 - Sunday Bloody Sunday

There have been two incidences in my Christian walk that have changed the course of my life and how I approach ministry. I write about both in this book. Ironically, they happened within a couple of years of each other. I'm a completely different person today because of it. Allow me to share the first life-changing event.

If you have never been told you might be dying, I highly recommend this experience. For me it was, in retrospect, a lifesaving and life-altering experience. Up until a few years ago, I was immortal. Death was a scary little troll that visited other people; but not me. I felt I had lived a somewhat charmed life. I had worked as a professional firefighter, a motorcycle was my mode of transportation, and I enjoyed hobbies that leaned towards the risky side. Never once did I really feel that I was close to the end.

But life has a funny way of reshuffling the deck and giving us all new cards to play.

I was dealt a new hand one Friday morning in a hospital room in Denver, Colorado, as several doctors made their way in to deliver their theories of my sudden illness. You see, over the previous four weeks, I had been putting on massive amounts of weight and experiencing swelling. I had already gone to one hospital; they misdiagnosed me and sent me home. I shrugged the whole thing off and was convinced that it would work itself out. It didn't.

One hundred pounds later, my caring wife and friends rolled me into a car and drove to Lutheran Medical Center on a Thursday evening. Twenty minutes later, I was told that I was in complete renal failure. My kidneys were no longer working, and the 100 plus pounds were actually water soaking into every crevice in my body, including my lungs.

"What?! Wait! I have never had any major health issues. Ever. I drink tons of water. I exercise. I don't smoke, and I wear my seat belt. I hug my kids, read my Bible, and not once have I killed a unicorn. Why me?" Of course, none of this information changed the fact that I was in bad shape.

And so on Friday morning, I was given their best guesses as to what was causing this health decline. The first and best outcome would be that I had a very rare type of syndrome. It was highly unlikely in people my age, but it was very treatable. I was hoping for this prognosis. Seeing the hope on my face, the doctors made sure to drive home the fact that it was statistically improbable. The other theories were less and less hopeful. One, in particular, got my attention because of the words they used. I was told it might be an aggressive form of cancer.

The word cancer sucks all by itself, but when you add the word "aggressive," it brings it to DEFCON 1. It's like being told you have a really gifted cancer. Yes, this cancer is smart. It takes all AP classes. It's really disciplined and focused on killing you quickly. How come I don't have the lazy cancer? "I'm sorry, Mr. Cheshire, but your cancer is passive aggressive. It's going to make a veiled shot at you, but will never come right out and attack you. Odds are, it will just hang out in your body."

Why can't I have **that** cancer? Nope, I may have the aggressive one. And so with these two likely scenarios, they needed to do a biopsy to find out what it was.

Later that afternoon, before the biopsy, I was informed that they would have the results sometime on Monday. With that, the blizzard of white coats filed out of my hospital room and I was alone again. It only took me a few minutes to realize I was going to be lying in this bed for three days with the idea of an early death marinating in my heart, head, and soul. I, of course, immediately thought of my three young kids and wife. I said over and over in my heart, "But I had so many more plans." It took a while to quiet my mind and do something productive. By that afternoon, I was making all kinds of lists: lists of my favorite things in life, lists of things I wanted to do if I didn't die. I made lists of the things I would improve as a husband, father, and friend. And then I came to my job.

I am a pastor. Anyone who does this job will attest to the massive highs and devastating lows you experience in walking out this calling. While making my list about church work, I discovered a rather large chip I had on my shoulder concerning my job. It was safe to say that the chip had moved from my shoulder to my heart. I realized that I carried a lot of anger about how Christians treated each other, myself included.

My memory was clogged with stories of relationship fallouts and the viciousness of feeding on each other.

So many times, we use Scriptures and twist them into "God's attack dogs." I, too, am very guilty of choosing to devour my brothers and sisters in the name of God, justice, and my rights. It was uncomfortable to realize that the idea of church for me, once so full of life, grace, and friendship had become a place of war, backbiting, and loss.

The message really hit home as I began to page through my journals from the previous ten years. I was amazed at all the friends I had lost over such petty things. Sometimes it was my fault. Sometimes it was theirs. But most of the time, it was a combination of misunderstandings and offenses. I kept thinking about the Rich Mullins song *We Are Not As Strong As We Think We Are*. One verse says, "It took the hand of God Almighty to part the waters in the sea, but it only took one little lie to separate you and me." Man, was he right!

We serve such a forgiving, loving, and accepting God; and yet, His church and His people seem to be angrier and more divided than ever before.

This isn't just my opinion either. I have had many talks with wonderful men and women of God who have noticed the slide towards Christian infighting and hate. In that hospital room, reading my old journals, I began to understand how easy it was for our enemy to divide us. I saw in myself the pettiness and bitterness that I had collected over years of being in ministry. I discovered how much unforgiveness and anger I had for people in my church, for how they had treated me, my family, my staff, and each other.

I may have been in the hospital with a kidney issue, but it was clear God was doing heart surgery on me. In fact, I began to rethink my career altogether. To be honest, by Sunday night, my wife, Amy, and I had decided that if God did give me more years to live then I wanted out of church work. In total disclosure, we decided we were done with going to church all together. We used the same logic every Christian leaves with; I don't need a church to have a relationship with God. My wife and I talked well into the early morning hours. We talked about other career paths I would take. We talked about the hurts we carried and even the ones we had caused. It was very cathartic. I instantly felt a massive wave of relief crash over me at the reality that I was done pastoring.

Like a dam that gave way, Amy and I started pouring out all the wonderful things that would come from leaving the ministry and never attending a church. Ahhh! We would no longer be responsible for anyone else's life but our own. No more giving half of our income to single moms and people who lost their jobs because the church is tapped out. We would use all our money to care for **our** kids and family and even buy toys like ATVs! Everyone else could go get help from some other place.

We could now defend ourselves when Christians were rude to us. We could talk openly about the movies we saw and which president we voted for. In fact, if we wanted, we could even vote for a party that Christians normally don't! Perhaps we wouldn't vote at all if we thought both the candidates were massive asses. Hey! We could use the word "asses" and it wouldn't affect our life! We would be able to discuss politics, religion, and church culture openly with our friends and not worry about offending entire people groups in church.

We could be proud that our kids go to public school, and simply walk away from the angry homeschooling mom that tells us we are a bad example to the body of Christ. We could now openly listen to music we like and I could even wear my Def Leppard t-shirt in public. Our kids would no longer need to hide their music selections and video games from church people because their opinions didn't matter. We wouldn't have to worry about what all the other churches and Christians in our city thought of us, because we would no longer be members or leaders. Now I could read the Bible for myself and not always be thinking of a sermon I have to build for others.

I'd get to watch all the football games on Sunday and not just the night games because I would no longer get stuck, after church, counseling the same couple who continually refuses to work on fixing things. I could use a few swear words without ruining my reputation or my "Christian witness." No, I wouldn't curse all the time, of course; I'd save it for a sporting event or for days that end with "Y." I could now openly be a fan of cage fighting without a lecture on violence.

Now, I have never done any jail time in my life, but I believe that what my wife and I felt that night is close to how a prisoner must feel when he walks out of prison after years behind bars . . . and baby, it was glorious! Like the movie *The Shawshank Redemption*, we had tunneled through a sewer to arrive on the other side free in Saywatanayo.

Monday morning, I had some of my core leaders come to my room and talked with them about ejecting from church and starting a business instead. I was leaving and they were all welcome to come with me or stay working at the church. They all wanted to come with me. We are not just a staff; we are best friends and have always wanted to do our life together. This honestly sounded way better than ministry.

You see where I'm going with this? When did outside of God's family become the place of peace and hope? And why was church a bad place to attend and an even worse place to serve?

About an hour after my staff left, the doctoral blizzard of white coats returned with the results. I was diagnosed with the rare type of Nephrotic Syndrome that people my age don't normally get, I was told that only 100 people in every million get it. The cause is unknown. I believe it's because I'm a high achiever. I really like to do things that others can't and sometimes that backfires. Take, for example, Jimi Heselden the tycoon who owned the Segway company, and died when he fell off a Segway from a 200 foot cliff. Some dreams end bad. But hey, I was going to be fine! I asked if they could just drain me like a Capri Sun; stab me with a straw and call me done! But from the onset of my illness, my heart had enlarged which meant we had to be careful taking the water out too fast. My doctor, who rocks by the way, told me this was a long process and that it would take several years to get completely restored. Getting the kidneys up and running again was a relatively quick fix. Within a few weeks, they were improving, but I'm still healing from the damage it caused to other parts of my body. I was so excited to be given more years to live, and I wasn't going to waste them. Amy was wiped out and went home to rest and I laid there smiling ear to ear.

Then another doctor walked in. God. I could feel Him want to discuss my plans, but I was not having it! "No way! I'm free now. I gave You a solid 15 years, God. It's time to let me enjoy life." I was expecting to hear Him say I was a bad person and that I didn't have any character. I was okay with what was coming, but God will always surprise you. He began to reason with me. He said He understood and just wanted to share His heart. He said, "It's all up to you, Michael."

Over the next few hours, I was given an education I will never forget. I can never forget. God began to free me to be who I was and still be a pastor. He encouraged me to try it again but do it as a real person this time around. Be authentic. God and I came to an understanding with each other. I would do ministry again, but this time I would be Michael, not Pastor Mike. I would challenge our church to be authentic, to be loving, to be kind. If a person was gossiping and hurting others, the leaders could say, "What's up with that? Not cool! Please stop." I would no longer care if people left over how my family, my staff, or I lived.

As a staff, we decided that even moral failures would not get you fired. If you said "sorry" and worked to fix what you broke with your bad behavior, then we wouldn't make you go sell shoes. God and I settled that if it all went south and everyone left, then at least I gave it the old college try. It's a funny thing about being a real, authentic, and grace-filled church. It's a little messy, but way easier. Sure, some people leave.

One couple walked out mid-sermon because I told our church to try to befriend the gays in our community, not to change them but to just understand them. They stormed out in a noticeable way. But the best part of that story, however, is that after making a little scene on the way out, they got to the car and realized she had left her purse under her chair. She sent her husband back in to fetch it. That gives a whole different meaning to the phrase, "Walk of Shame."

I began to find real passion in teaching and leading my team again, something I had lost. And the church began to grow. I mean **really** grow. I was now part of the church and not just the leader. The Church has to be the church for the leaders, too. You see, my experience is not unique. Nor is it confined to those in ministry.

Today, there are so many Christians leaving the church in America just to find the freedom from religion's harsh glare. In truth, so many are leaving all at once that it is hard to accurately track the numbers. Even with the facts staring us in the face, many Christians, and even leaders, keep denying there is any type of problem. And if that is you, then you really won't be able to handle what I'm about to say in this chapter, much less this book. Perhaps you should walk away from this book now, because what I'm going to cover will be damaging to your special brand of Christian mythology.

You see, if we are to deal with the real problems in our churches, we must first accept the hard fact that they really are problems.

If my wife and I are going to bed and a snake quickly slithers across the floor and under our bed, we won't simply deny it's there just because we can't see it. We got a glimpse, and now we must do what any other normal adult would do, which is scream like a little girl and run to get weapons! Maybe something heavy and pointy, but nothing from the Nerf family, to be sure. If we can't find it after we've returned with our artillery, we will do the next logical thing: burn the house down. All kidding aside, we will not be able to rest in that house until the danger is gone.

The data on just how many Christians are leaving is increasingly tough to collect due, in part, to the way these guys go bye-bye. When the hurt, tired, or disillusioned Christ-followers leave, they rarely bolt. Instead, they tend to fade out of view. They miss church here and there. Three or four weeks go by. They stop giving, serving, and eventually their absence goes unnoticed. I don't even think that's really the leadership's fault, as much as the Christians in the church are not genuinely developing friendships within our congregations.

People will fade out of a church, a club, or a movement. But people don't fade out of their friendships; friends would notice and come after them. Yes, the mass exodus from our churches is continuing and spreading. Those leaving, for the most part, are not mad at God, His requirements or His duties.

Despite what you will hear from some religious leaders in today's church culture, the average Christ-follower walking out the door is not weak, unwilling to be committed, or intrinsically selfish.

The vast majority of these Christians are leaving for two main reasons: First, and foremost, they are tired of being treated harshly by other Christians. Second, they feel the church has lost relevance to its community and to what they are going through in their everyday lives.

Sure, I agree with the argument that there are many churches that bring real relevance to our faith. But the way we treat each other within our faith communities is still stunningly bad, and in many ways, out of control. Anyone can find out why an entire generation is leaving church without an in-depth study.

It's all hidden in conversations with the very people who have left.

I spent this last year having hundreds of conversations with great Christians who have hung up the towel of church attendance and moved on. I actually placed an ad on Craigslist to interview some, and literally, boatloads answered. Most were in their late twenties and early thirties. They were more than willing to meet for coffee and share their hearts. I found out some surprising things.

Most missed attending a local church, not enough to go back, but many felt a longing to try it again. I found that they were, overall, not really bitter or angry at the church, but admitted to being happier now and felt more authentic about their faith in Christ. One of the most startling things I discovered was they almost all shared their faith way more with their friends since leaving church. When they weren't trying to close the salvation deal, their conversations just flowed.

During this time with my de-churched friends, I always liked to end with a question about what it would take to get them to plug in again to a local church. The answers almost all centered around two things: One was that they would have to see a church actively do real things in and for their community without being pushy about attending their church. And second, they would need to be convinced that the Christians in that church were nice. That is the very word they used most. Nice. We must be nicer.

Funny. It almost feels like a word we only use on children. "Be nice" or "Someone's not playing nice!" We simply are not being nice to each other. What a great word! Too many Christians run around being the opposite of nice. Mean. They try to force and push fellow Christians to live exactly like them, parent like them, do marriage like them, eat like them, exercise like them, talk like them, vote like them, and despise the same people as them.

Honestly, it's like the church is going through some kind of clone war. At moments like these, I can't help but think of Anne Lamott's great quote, "You can tell you have created God in your own image when it turns out He hates all the same people you hate." Yikes! It's true we have lost the art of simply being nice to each other.

Now please allow me to speak openly and honestly with you for a moment. Please don't just check out because I may say a thing or two you disagree with. One of the reasons we continue down a divided road is because we can't seem to have honest dialogue anymore without getting mad and turning it into an argument or checking out of the discussion all together.

I think we can choose to be not so thin-skinned, if only for a few hours. So let's expose the last, ugly 10 percent of our internal war.

It starts with the leaders and then gets picked up in the pews. We aren't so much the body of Christ anymore as we are a civil war. We have become consumed with infighting, judgments, and pointless debates. We can discount every movement, denomination, and church with broad judgments. It's like Christianity's own brand of racism and discrimination. Maybe you have even heard some for yourself: The Seeker Church doesn't disciple people, the Teaching Church doesn't reach the lost, the Mega Church is about the show. The Little Church is focused inward. The House Church is a joke. The seminarians are too educated to relate to everyday people, and the pastors with no theological training are heretics.

We rip each other up over theology and arguments that can never truly be totally understood this side of Heaven. Christian leaders have debated these issues for years, and in the end, they don't really affect any of the instructions Jesus has given us. And as the leader goes, so goes everyone else.

The homeschooled kids will have social issues, the public school kids will sleep around, the mother who works a job is uncaring and inattentive, the mother who stays home is lucky she doesn't have to work. Those who watch R-rated movies are worldly; those who watch only G-rated movies are legalistic. If you drink beer or wine, you're a drunk. If you don't drink, you're a prude. If you vote for a Democrat, you are a baby killer. If you vote for a Republican, you hate poor people. If you get involved with social justice, you're a Humanist. If you don't, you're self-centered. On and on and on it goes. Oh, how the mediocre have fallen!

So why this book? Why not this book?! It's not like being honest about our issues is going to make things worse. I firmly believe that by finally dragging our differences and petty arguments into the light of day, it will be a massive first step in breaking our mean habits. For far too long, while we have been waging a war within our own foxholes, the real enemy has had the run of the place. He has been unchallenged because Christ's army is too wounded from friendly fire to even crawl to the battlefield for the real fight. And an enemy who is unopposed is no longer your enemy. He has actually become your ruler.

Jesus spoke very clearly to this issue when he said that a house divided could not stand. And so here we are on the ground, but we don't have to stay there. I believe in the Church that Christ established. I believe it's possible to find our way back into relevance and purpose within our communities again. I believe we can serve ourselves right back into a major role in our country. When we start filling the holes in our community that no one else wants to fill, we will see a shift in momentum.

What would happen if Christians took the little league coaching positions that no one has time to? What would happen if Christians volunteered at the library and read to the children and the elderly? What if Christians learned CPR and offered to teach people for free? What would happen if Christians volunteered to paint the schools for free during the summer to bring relief to our already stressed school budgets? What would happen if the Christians served at the local pound or homeless shelter? What if we worked in the volunteer corps? What if we took time to write letters to our church leaders, police, firemen, veterans, and teachers to let them know they are loved?

What if we found ways to use our church buildings during the week for our community instead of letting them sit empty all week? What if churches use what they are good at to help another church grow stronger in a weak area? What if your church web guys could help teach the other churches how to manage their page better? What if, as church leaders, we begin to kill our pride and call other churches for wisdom on how to improve instead of convincing ourselves we know everything?

Most churches want to attract teens, but many are stuck in what worked 20 years ago. If you build a youth center and fill it with old couches, a foosball table and a bunch of Lionel Richie records, then you need a hug. Call a church that attracts kids and ask them for ideas. If they refuse to help. . .stalk them, pester them. Guilt them.

Go watch the movie *What About Bob?* and act like the other churches are Dr. Leo Marvin and you are Bob. You may find other churches are actually flattered that you asked. What would happen if we gave our church trade secrets away so other churches don't have to learn the hard lessons on their own? If all that started happening in a community, I'll tell you what would happen: The Church would matter.

But for all that to happen, we must first love each other. Jesus said that someday the world would know we were His disciples, not by the way we loved Him, but rather by the way we love each other. For some of us, we are going to be the change. I, for one, don't want to be a leader that presided over the worst disintegration of the Church in history. I would rather not have to explain that to God when I give an account for my life.

And so this book is my first cannon shot. I am in a pretty unique position as a pastor, writer, and Christian leader. Much like Pinocchio, "I've got no strings . . ." Because of the church I serve in and the leaders around me, I can be blunt and honest about this stuff without the worry of getting fired by denominational leaders or a board. I have no funding that I can lose. I have found myself in a position in my life where I own my own publishing and marketing company that is doing very well. And as the founder and owner, editors have a hard time telling me what I can't say. I don't have to run my heart through test groups, standards and practices, or any type of church political correctness.

I am also well aware that this book is going to bring me more critics than I already have. This is always good with me. Hey, if you're not being criticized, then you're not trying. I already have a following of several with whom I interact. They let me know that I'm really going to Hell, and I inform them that Katy Perry says that I'm a firework. We are working tirelessly on getting them a sense of humor, but it's pretty slow going.

One final thought: This book does not hold all the answers of how to get Christians to stop hurting each other. It is, however, a discussion and not meant to be a book at all. *Why We Eat Our Own* is just a mere collection of thoughts, ideas, revelations, insights, and observations. It's really a tour of my soul during my own spiritual journey. This book doesn't really flow either. I didn't write it with that purpose in mind. I change gears a lot and rarely use the clutch. I tried to talk to everyone involved about this issue of us hurting each other. Whether you are a leader, attendee, defector, critic, victim, or perpetrator, this a conversation for you.

So let's get started because people are hungry and we need to find another food source than eating each other. How about we kill some of our sacred cows for the first course?

According to the World Christian Encyclopedia Published in 2001, more than 1,200 different Christian denominations exist in the United States alone.

Appetizers

To fogive is necessary and required,
but to restore is the stuff that makes kings.

#WhyWeEatOurOwn

#why we eat our own 2

Going To Hell With Ted Haggard

"So this is where you fell, and I am left to sell,
The path to heaven runs through miles of clouded hell,
Right to the top, don't look back"
Imagine Dragons - It's Time

I didn't plan to care about Ted Haggard. After all, I had access to Google and a Bible. I heard about what he did and knew it was wrong. I saw the clips from the news and the HBO documentary about his life after his fall. I honestly felt bad for him, but figured it was his own undoing. When the topic came up with others I know in ministry, we would feign sadness, but inside we could care less. One close friend said he would understand it more if Ted had just sinned with a woman. I agreed with him at the time. It's amazing how much more mercy I give to people who struggle with sins I understand. The further their sin is from my own personal struggles, the more judgmental and callous I become. I'm not proud of that. It's just where I was at that time in my walk. But that all changed in one short afternoon.

Eating our own

A while back, I was having a business lunch at a sports bar in the Denver area with a close atheist friend. He's a great guy and a very deep thinker. During lunch, he pointed at the large TV screen on the wall. It was set to a channel recapping Ted's fall. He pointed his finger at the HD and said, "That is the reason I will not become a Christian. Many of the things you say make sense, Mike, but that's what keeps me away."

It was well after the story had died down, so I had to study the screen to see what my friend was talking about. I assumed he was referring to Ted's hypocrisy. "Hey man, not all of us do things like that," I responded. He laughed and said, "Michael, you just proved my point. See, that guy said sorry a long time ago. Even his wife and kids stayed and forgave him, but all you Christians still seem to hate him. You guys can't forgive him and let him back into your good graces. Every time you talk to me about God, you explain that he will take me as I am. You say he forgives all my failures and will restore my hope, and as long as I stay outside the church, you say God wants to forgive me. But that guy failed while he was one of you, and most of you are still vicious to him." Then he uttered words that left me reeling: "You Christians eat your own. Always have. Always will."

Change of heart

He was running late for a meeting and had to take off. I, however, could barely move. I studied the TV and read the caption as a well-known religious leader kept shoveling dirt on a man who had admitted he was unclean. And at that moment, my heart started to change. I began to distance myself from my previously harsh statements and tried to understand what Ted and his family must have been through. When I brought up the topic to other men and women I love and respect, the very mention of Haggard's name made our conversations toxic. Their reactions were visceral.

Please understand, this isn't just my experience. Just Google his name and read what is said about him in Christian circles. Most Christians would say God can forgive him, but almost universally people agree that God will never use him again. When I pressed the question, "Why can't God still use Ted?" I was dismissed as foolish or silly. Most of these people got mad and demanded I drop the subject. Perhaps they saw something I was missing, but this response seemed strange. After all, I reasoned, Jesus restored Peter after he denied Christ. That's a pretty big deal. And what about the Scripture that teaches us that the gifts and callings of God are irrevocable? So I felt I needed to meet Ted for myself. So I had my assistant track him down for a lunch appointment. I live outside Denver and he was living in Colorado Springs, a little over an hour away. Perfect!

We exchanged a few emails and agreed on a date and a restaurant. I took two men from my staff, and we met him for lunch. All the way there, I quietly played out in my head how he would act. Would he be reserved? Sad? Angry or distant?

Surprised by friendship

In less than five minutes of talking with Ted, I realized a horrible truth—I liked him. He was brutally honest about his failures. He was excited that the only people who would talk to him now were the truly broken and hurt. During our conversation a lady approached him. He instantly went into "pastor mode" and cared for her. Deep inside God was teaching me that true salvation is an ongoing process. We spent two hours together and decided to stay in touch. I began to call and ask him church-related questions. He possesses a wealth of wisdom. He even has a growing church in the very city that knows him for his biggest failures. I thought I had it tough as a church planter! But God is causing his church to really grow. I met his wonderful wife, Gayle. She is a terrific teacher of grace and one of my heroes. When I grow up, I want to be Gayle Haggard. And so, I became close friends with Ted Haggard.

But then the funniest thing started happening to me. Some Christians I hung out with told me they would distance themselves from me if I continued reaching out to Ted. Several people in my church said they would leave. Really? Does he have leprosy? Will he infect me? We are friends. We aren't dating! But in the end, I was told that my voice as a pastor and author would be tarnished if I continued to spend time with him. I found this sickening. Not just because people can be so small, but because I have a firsthand account from Ted and Gayle of how they lost many friends they had known for years. Much of it is pretty cold-blooded. Now the "Christian machine" was trying to take away their new friends.

It would do some Christians good to stay home one weekend and watch the entire DVD collection of HBO's, *Band of Brothers*. Marinate in it. Take notes. Write down words like loyalty, friendship, and sacrifice.

Understand the phrase: never leave a fallen man behind.

Where's the love?

I had a hard time understanding why we as Christians really needed Ted to crawl on the altar of church discipline and die. We needed a clean break. He needed to do the noble thing and walk away from the church. He needed to protect our image. When Ted crawled off that altar and into the arms of a forgiving God, we chose to kill him with our disdain. I wrestled with my part in this, until I got an epiphany. In a quiet time of prayer, Christ revealed to me a brutal truth: it was my fault. We are called to leave the 99 to go after the one. We are supposed to be numbered with the outcasts. After all, we are the ones that believe in resurrection. In many ways, I have not been aggressive enough with the application of the gospel. My concept of grace needed to mature, to grow muscles, get teeth, and acquire bad breath. It needed to carry a shield, and most of all, it needed to find its voice.

Grace must pick a side in the light of day, not just whisper its opinion in the shadows and dark places where we sign our name, Anonymous. When a leader falls and then repents, grace picks a side. Grace is strong. Grace is a shield to those who cannot get off the battlefield. Grace is God's idea. Like a spiritual Switzerland, we stay in our neutral world where we can both forgive and judge but never get our hands dirty caring for the fallen. And when we don't pick a side, the wrong side gets picked for us. Crematoriums are more sanitary than hospitals. Let's change this!

Of course, I understand that if a person doesn't repent, there is not a whole lot you can offer. But Ted resigned, confessed, repented, and submitted. He jumped through our many hoops. When will we be cool with him again? When will the church allow God to use him again? It's funny that we believe we get to make that decision.

The Ted Haggard issue reminds me of a scene in Mark Twain's, *Huckleberry Finn*. Huck is told that if he doesn't turn in his friend, a runaway slave named Jim, he will surely burn in hell. So one day Huck, not wanting to lose his soul to Satan, writes a letter to Jim's owner telling her of Jim's whereabouts. After folding the letter, he starts to think about what his friend has meant to him, how Jim took the night watch so he could sleep, how they laughed and survived together. Jim is his friend and that is worth the reconsideration. Huck realizes that it's either Jim's friendship or hell. Then the great Mark Twain writes such wonderful words of resolve. Huck rips the paper and says, "All right then, I guess I'll go to hell."

What a great lesson. What a great attitude. I think of John 15:13, "Greater love has no one than this: to lay down one's life for one's friends." Maybe it's not just talking about our physical life. Perhaps it's the life we know, the friends we have and lose. Maybe I show love when I lay down the life we have together to confront you on a wrong attitude or action. Maybe we show no greater love than when we are counted with people who others consider tainted. Becoming friends with Ted was a defining moment in my life, ministry, and career. Sure, I lost a few relationships, but I doubt they would have cared for me in my failures. So really, I lost nothing. If being Ted's friend causes some to hate and reject me—all right then, I guess I'll go to hell.

That last sentence was where that chapter was supposed to end. In the course of working on this book, parts of chapters got picked up and published in some Christian magazines and online publications. *Going to Hell with Ted Haggard* was among them. When it went public, things got a little crazy. In the weeks and months following its release, our church was hit with literally thousands of email, calls, and Facebook messages concerning what was written. I was expecting some angry critics to tell me how God and the church could forgive Ted, but that he had disqualified himself from service. And those guys definitely showed up.

They recycled the same arguments about making grace cheap and that leaders are held to a higher standard. Some of their positions were so insane, it was actually entertaining. "If we love, accept, and restore Ted and he is allowed to be a pastor again, then pastors everywhere will begin sinning because they can get away with it." Hey, I got bad news, my fellow Christians, pastors everywhere sin because we do get away with it. Some of us are just way better at hiding it.

Hundreds of people said "I didn't know the whole story." Well maybe that's true. Maybe. But I made calls to those intimately involved about how the Haggards were treated, and I never got a return call or an answered email. I made it clear I was not going to make anyone look bad, but all that was returned was their silence. I just wanted to see if we could learn to do this kind of thing a little less brutally.

Ironically, as soon as the article came out, a few of those people did reach out to me. They were happy I didn't make them or their ministry look bad. I guess in ministry, image control is, at times, a more powerful god than the silly little things Jesus taught. In the end, my heart just wasn't wanting to get in the same room with people who only talk from a place of fear for their reputation.

We got a few emails that were just plain toxic.

They were mostly anonymous in nature or signed with names that seemed too simple. I mean, how many John Smiths are really out there anyway? And what are the odds they all hate Ted Haggard?

Hey, let me give some of you information that maybe you don't know. My church runs several businesses, including some that involve pretty advanced technical computer skills. You might be surprised how fast a 24-year-old (with mad computer skills and a Slurpee) can legally track down who you really are, Mr. Anonymous.

Some of them made it too easy. A few of the critics forgot to turn off their Auto Signature. So after signing "anonymous," I got nine ways to contact them via Twitter handle, Facebook page, and one lady even had a pager number! I didn't even know people still used pagers. All I'm saying is that it's sad that Christians can't even do judgmental things well anymore. I mean, come on, guys! If we aren't going to be loving, let's hate with excellence!

Honestly, I feel our churches and their internal governing mechanisms, for the most part, are not really designed to even know how to start the restoration process for their leaders. We traffic more in "store-ation" then restoration. We simply pack up failed leaders and set them adrift when they are at their lowest. In many cases, we have them sign contracts on the way out saying that they will get some severance pay, but only if the offerings stay up, or all bets are off.

Sometimes when I talk to a leader, who is in this process, I think back to the scene in the movie *Raiders of The Lost Ark*. At the end of the movie, Indiana Jones is asking the government official, "Who is studying the ark and where is it?" But they just keep saying that they have top men working on it. And then, they cut to a scene of it being nailed in a crate and pushed to the back of a giant warehouse full of other similar crates. The idea is that it would be left there, hidden forever.

They did this in the movie because the Ark was unpredictable and possibly dangerous. Much like a hurt and fallen church leader, we worry about how this will all play out. Maybe it's the risk that makes churches send the fallen leaders away to let our church body "heal" from their sin. We have fallen a long way from the example Jesus set in being numbered with the outcast.

Look, I'm not saying I have all the answers. Perhaps, it's just my job to ask the question: Could a pastor fall and be lovingly restored in the same church to the same position and the church actually grow from it? I don't know, but I would attend any church that committed to grace and love.

Truth is, the vast majority of people who reached out to us had really resonated with the idea of raw grace. Many even said that the article changed their mind about leaders who fall. Wow!

When we all start rethinking things and asking the hard questions, maybe we will actually learn from our missteps.

To this day, I am friends with Ted and Gayle. Not a week goes by that we don't talk several times. We have lunch every other week to talk "shop" and discuss the Grace Round Tables that have really exploded as a movement. I use the time to steal great insights from Gayle, and we laugh a lot. Even as I write this, Ted just called because he may need to find places to house some of his church members who are being evacuated due to a massive fire in Colorado Springs.

Ted's out there doing it! He's loving and caring just like so many other pastors. He's doing what he was designed to do and his church is growing because of it. There will always be some Christians who believe Ted and Gayle should never do ministry again. But now there are a lot of us on the other side saying that he must stand back up and serve again. Until Ted Haggard is accepted and loved again, as a brother and leader in the body of Christ, then our cute little sermons on Christ's redemptive and restorative power are no betterthan Greek mythology.

Appetizers

-The more friends you have, the less likely you are to suffer from insomnia or chronic fatigue.

-If a friendship lasts longer than seven years, psychologists say it will last a lifetime.

Love with hidden agendas is not love.
There is a word for that,
it's called manipulation
#WhyWeEatOurOwn

why we eat our own 3

Head Games & Heart Problems

"If they could love like you and me,
Imagine what the world could be,
If everyone cared and nobody cried,
If everyone loved and nobody lied,
If everyone shared and swallowed their pride,
Then we'd see the day when nobody died"
Nickelback - If Everyone Cared

Recently, I was watching a TV program about Rapa Nui, or as it is better known, Easter Island. Many of us would know it as the small (only 66 square miles) Polynesian island in the Pacific Ocean that has giant ancient heads assembled along the shorelines. The heads are called Moai. I have always wondered what the story was behind them, and so I did extensive research on the real history of Easter Island and found an explanation as to why the Moai were made and what happened to the people.

To my surprise, I found out that for quite some time, historians honestly didn't know why it all happened. Researchers have been studying the remnants, of this once great civilization, for many years now and have finally arrived at a theory for the abrupt ending to such peaceful people. And, boy, did their story hit home for me when I consider what is going on in our churches these days. Allow me to share with you the story and then perhaps we can find the lines of relevance. The narrative goes something like this:

From archaeological digs around the island, they know it was once covered in trees. What is also revealed is that at the height of the island's thriving existence, there were five tribes (totaling well over 20,000 inhabitants). These tribes all got along just fine, even participating in island-wide festivals together. Trees played a critical role in the livelihood of the natives who made canoes out of the giant palm trees to support fishing operations.

This was predominantly a fishing community so fish was obviously the main food source for every man, woman and child. Using boats to spread nets offshore brought in enough food for the entire island easily. As you might expect, the life span of a wooden boat made out of non-pressure treated wood was short. After six months to a year, a boat would have to be retired and recycled into a hut roof, a bucket or simply used as firewood. This was never an issue since trees were abundant and there was always a new tree ready to be hollowed out and put into service.

Then, somewhere in this time of great abundance, one of the tribes decided to carve a stone monument honoring an elder leader who had passed away. As Moai go, it was quite unimpressive really, standing at under four feet tall. Upon completion, it was rolled to the shoreline and faced inland. He watched over their people. The people believed the sea was the other world or heaven. A Moai facing away from the sea meant it was watching over and sending favor to the people of the village, their land, fishing, health, and commerce. This practice of honor and superstition soon began to spread to the other tribes around the island. Thus, the trees began to serve an added duty as rollers to move the increasingly bigger and bigger Moai from the quarry to the seashore and their final resting place. After the sculpting was done, the Moai was placed on its back and positioned on makeshift rollers to move these mammoth heads slowly to the sea. Scientists say that the average Moai weighs 14 tons, so you can understand how that would shred wooden logs pretty fast. Not to worry though, the island had plenty of trees.

Over time, people began to make the heads bigger and bigger. One good theory was that by making them larger, the people would show more honor to their elders, gods, spirits, or whatever. At least it would show up the tribe down the road. Being competitive in nature, other tribes responded to the bigger Moai by taking it up to the next level themselves.

Rather quickly, a push to show more spirituality by making the bigger more powerful gods became the island's main occupation. Remember, the first Moai started off small at under four feet and the largest one recorded measured at over 71 feet tall and weighing in at a stunning 165 tons. What a monstrosity! That one actually never made it to the sea. In fact, the entire Moai making operation came to a sudden and screeching halt. Of the 887 Moai, only 288 are at their proper spots. Ninety-two were stopped in the middle of transit, and 397 are still laying in the Ran Raraku quarry.

But why? It's very simple; there were no more trees to transport them. In truth, there were no more trees for anything. No trees to make boats and catch fish. No more trees to build huts or buckets, to burn for fire or to make bows and arrows. The island, to this very day, looks bald and barren, but hundreds of years ago, it was lush and full with a canopy of all variations of trees. So with the depletion of such a critical resource, people began to move into caves for shelter and look for food where they could. The island, once a huge nesting ground for birds, soon lost its feathery friends as the birds began to realize they were next on the menu. Ultimately, they used their wings to relocate to islands that were less hostile.

Thus, it came to be that thousands of people began to starve. In starving, they turned their attention to the only other source of food on the island . . . each other. A great people who once lived in peace, intermarried and celebrated together, now brutally hunted each others' husbands, wives and children for food. They turned cannibalistic.

Their consciences had been seared away and replaced by a new inner law of self-preservation. And if history has taught us anything, it is this: that the pursuit of self always turns humanity into dark, evil animals. Where there was once a loving community of people, chaos and murder reigned, becoming a real nightmare from which they would never awaken. And all of this pain is credited to the mad dash to build their spirituality bigger than their neighbor, to show the other tribes that they had more truth, a bigger god, a better protection plan. In the end, this once very great people and land died. The island was void of life, people and hope.

I bet some of you are starting to see where I'm going with this. You see, we have to start asking ourselves the motive questions again. Many of the decisions in our life and even in our churches can seem great and godly, but if it's out of the wrong heart, we may be sowing some nightmare situations into our future. To better understand this, let me share a few stories I came across during my time planning this book.

A while back, I was talking to a guy at a conference who was explaining that his church had restored one of their high level leaders after he had a moral issue come to light. I was beyond happy to hear about a success story because in my time of research, I had heard of so few that ended well. I asked if I could buy him lunch and interview him. He agreed, and I sat down with him and a few of his younger staff for an hour during the lunch break. It seemed like they really had it together, and I was blown away at how simple he made it sound. After our time together, he had to leave to go home early and I stayed at the conference.

After the final session, I was approached by one

of the young men who had been with us at lunch. He asked if I had a second, and we stepped out a door that led to the back parking lot. He said, "That's not the real story, just so you know." He went on to tell me that he had another friend who worked for the church a few years before in the youth department. The young man was caught at church looking at porn and fired on the spot. He was asked to leave the body so that the kids could see that sin has consequences. I was stunned. The other pastor was handled more graciously. Then he "Paul Harvey-ed" me with "the rest of the story."

He told me the guy they restored was, indeed, on staff and a pastor but was not paid. He, in fact, was very wealthy and, by far, the biggest giver in church. The young man told me that if they had dealt with him the way they dealt with that youth pastor, the church would have lost a ton of money. He added one great thought towards the end of our little private meeting by saying, "I guess in the end, my friend just didn't bring enough value to the table of grace." I thought that was a very powerful statement.

My mind, of course, runs back to the Scripture where James tells the church to be very careful about showing favorites. He tells them that if you see a person with a nice big ring (a sign of wealth) on their hand, bring him to the front (a place of honor) but ask the poor person to go sit in the back, "you have discriminated among yourselves and become judges with evil thoughts." I asked what his friend was doing now and he said he had left church all together and works in teaching the newly blind. He said, "He believes what he did disqualified him for ministry."

And with that display of spiritual discipline, another tree is worn away under the weight of appearances.

What could he have been if grace, mercy and help were offered? Is it any wonder why many churches are in decline when we keep firing all the young men and women God is raising up? So they have sin and flaws. Chances are they will do something wrong and your precious church name will take a hit. Can we not start to see their value again through the eyes of Christ?

Hey ministry friends, can I speak to you all for a second here? Look, I'm a pastor, and I am all too aware of the pressure to get the money to pay bills and do all the outreach we need to do. I understand the desire to keep key donors, but honestly, sometimes even the rich Christians in our churches need a kick in the pants. I often tell our church that, for some of them, it's too easy to write a check. They need to keep their money sometimes and get their hands dirty caring for others. And just maybe the poor need to be treated like they are just as valuable as the millionaires among us.

Leaders, if you're afraid of losing those with money then you're never going to be the kind of leader God made you to be. I can't count how many times we have offered to give people back their money because they tried using it as a tool of control. Most of the time, they see what they were doing and how wrong it was; but several times, we have cut checks for thousands and said bye-bye. God ALWAYS, ALWAYS, ALWAYS replaces it. Take that to the bank.

Too many of our decisions in church, I feel, are made because we have a mortgage to pay and need things to move along with financial ease. I have read many contracts that churches made newly-fired pastors sign agreeing to receive severance only if the church giving stayed up. "If it goes down at all, we will blame you and terminate your final pay, in Jesus' name. Amen." So I ask you, who are we really serving?

This has all got to stop. So we lose a building or a few hundred people for standing up for the sinners in our midst. At the end of the day, maybe the hyperfocus on a balanced budget is unbalancing our hearts. And for all my wealthy Christian friends out there, don't think that because you have more cash that you're all-knowing about how a church should spend it.

I can't stand it when loaded people buy vans,

sound equipment and stuff we never asked for and bring it to church. I tell them, "That's hijacking the budget." I know they truly believe they mean well, but our church staff team has a better view of the needs. A great pair of speakers is great for service but it can't help the newly single mom pay her rent this month. These days, I will always just sell it. Sounds harsh? Oh well.

Our church is in a war for people's forevers and that means, in our little world, we will use the things God brings in the best ways we can. Don't donate your great-grandmother's quilted blanket to our church unless you're okay with it being given to an out of work, former soldier who is struggling to make peace with the things he has seen and done. Don't donate a dollar if you don't want it to go to help pay the counseling bill for a new Christian woman who is still struggling with cutting herself. Don't donate your old car if you're not okay with us crushing it for scrap and using the money to buy more rafts for our youth group. Our mission to care and love tends to change what we see value in. Okay. I feel better now. * Exit soap box *

But church leadership is only part of the issue. The stuff that goes on in the pews is just as motive-driven as well. A lot of church-goers can drift into a cliquish behavior. It's really common in every organization for certain people to pull together and create a tight community within a community; however, when you get exclusive in a church, you're doing church wrong.

I got an email from a woman in another state explaining her story of why she and her husband hadn't been to a church in 14 years. Both of them were very active in their small local church and had a great friendship with three other families there. Everything was fine until their only son turned 15 and became pretty rebellious. He went on to make repeatedly bad decisions over the next year or so, and as that went on, they noticed that they were being left out of more and more get-togethers with their church friends. Understand that this kid wasn't killing people; he was skipping school a lot and got caught with drugs several times. The story culminated one night while picking up dinner. On the way home, she and her husband passed the local bowling alley and noticed all their friends' cars in the parking lot. They stopped and decided to see what was going on. She said that when they walked in, they could feel the awkwardness. She asked one of the women why they were not invited and was told that the group didn't want their kids to be seen with her son because it might give the appearance that they were approving of his behavior. They didn't want to ask them to leave their son at home because they felt it would be hurtful, so instead they chose to leave them out of events as a family until the son was "under control."

Needless to say, the friendships were left in a broken pile of hurt somewhere on lane eight of the local bowling alley. She said if they had just told them their concerns, they could have worked it out. She understood they didn't want a bad influence around their kids, but to shun them was just too much. That was the last time they attended a church. They just felt so hurt. The local pastor tried to get hold of them, but they simply told him they wanted to be left alone with no explanation.

Incidentally, the kid turned out just fine. After several more issues, he got his head on straight. She said he joined the military for a few years and after his service, began working his way into management at a great company. He is a strong Christian, has a wife, two kids and spends one weekend a month working with "at risk" kids. He also encouraged his parents to go back to church and forgive the people for their silliness. I guess you cannot always judge a book by its adolescence.

It's so sad how many friendships are lost on the Altar of Appearance. Way too often, I hear similar stories. I must admit that both sides could have made better and bolder decisions to press in and work toward a real relationship. But I can't help but think somewhere along the way, we have to see that in the mad dash to look like appropriate Christians, we are starting to look like just mean-spirited animals.

When we let friendships and community slip out of our hands without a real fight to hold onto them, we become just like those Moai movers. And we don't realize that the things of real value are being chewed up under the giant images of our perceived spirituality. We can talk all day about discipleship, theology, methodology and missions within the church, but if we cannot get true friendship and loyalty back in our hearts and lives, then we will continue to be a divided people who know less and less about driving out the darkness and more and more about how to throw people under the bus.

Appetizers

Although Easter Island was once desolate, the population has begun to grow.

Currently, the island has a population of 5,761.

Anyone can find fault. It's the cheapest gift of all.
Find the answer. That's what the world needs!
#Why We Eat Our Own

#why we eat our own 4

Why I Always Give Money To The Homeless

A Few Thoughts On Judgmentalism

"Your values is a disarray, prioritizing horribly,
Unhappy with your riches,
'cause you're piss poor morally,
Ignoring all prior advice and forewarning,
And we mighty full of ourselves, all of a sudden aren't we?"
T.I. - Live Your Life

The ability to find faults in others is really the cheapest gift of all.

As a church leader, when I ask myself why we Christians eat our own, the first people group I think of is the judgmental Christians. And so, I would like to talk directly to you Christians who are judgmental towards others in the body of Christ, but I'm also addressing those outside the church as well.

I just want to reason with you. . . . Unfortunately, I cannot, because to this day, I have never, not one time, met a truly judgmental person who has admitted to it and owned it. In my time in church and around Christianity, I have seen my fair share of judgmental folks. But if there is one unifying characteristic about them all, it is that they will always vehemently deny being judgmental.

In fact, if you have ever admitted to being judgmental, my guess is you are really just a normal Christian. Look, we may not all be judgmental, but we are definitely all carriers. We will have moments when we have to catch ourselves looking down on people and need to adjust our hearts accordingly. But when a Christian goes into judgmental lock down for good, they become a destructive force to both themselves and others.

They will start using catch phrases to excuse their brand of justice. Things like, "I'm just telling it like it is." They will also try to use Scriptures to explain why they are not really doing anything wrong in being mean and critical.

I have heard people say they have a prophetic gift. This is often Christian code for "I'm mean and rude to others, but it's how God made me. Because, you know, the prophets were tough." Sure, I'll agree to that. But to be fair, they were also hunted and killed quite often. They had to develop a special kind of bold, terse communication style because people often threw rocks at them a lot.

Let's not pretend we are being persecuted in this nation. I mean, come on guys! Really? We are going to play this card? Are we really going to try to spin our reality into something it's not? You can have your conspiracy theories about how our government is secretly coming after churches and Christians, how "the man" has a covert, well-organized plan for taking all our rights away.

Look, don't let my crude vocabulary and lack of writing skills fool you. I'm actually very well read and have an IQ in the triple digits, so there are not a lot of words I don't understand. Because of that I can say with full confidence that if our government is working together to come after us . . . we've got plenty of time. Have you seen what's going on over in Washington lately? They can't agree on anything or get one real meaningful law passed. Now you tell me some of those guys are working together to bring us all down? I think we will win that battle. In fact, after seeing how they organize stuff. I think we would even cover the point spread.

Heck, they make our churches look like well-oiled machines. The most persecution my pastor friends or I will feel as ministers in this country might happen on the 15th hole of a golf course . . . when our cell service drops to only two bars. Perhaps we shouldn't compare ourselves to men and women who were beaten, boiled, burned, drowned, and fed to lions. I'll accept the "I'm a prophet and rough around the edges" from them but not from American Christians whose lattes were not as foamy as it was for the atheists. So maybe we can dispense with the argument that the Christian prophetic voice in this country needs to be mean. No, there is no excuse for being a judgmental Christian; however, there are reasons.

You see, judgmental Christians are made not born. People become judgmental because their parents were consistently critical of others. It's amazing the things our children absorb.

Sometimes, a person gets emotionally damaged, and never heals correctly. Often, they can develop a critical spirit in order to protect themselves from being further damaged. There are many reasons Christians become this way, but I will always believe the biggest reason is insecurity. And where does insecurity come from?

Failure can be a wonderful teacher, but sometimes she kills her students.

Consider a loving Christian woman in a typical Christian marriage with two little girls. She is so kind and honestly cares about people in a real authentic way. However, after 10 years of marriage, she comes home from a Saturday morning workout and her husband tells her he is leaving her for another woman.

Funny thing about the typical life; it can instantly get very untypical. She cries, she pleads, she will do whatever it takes, but he won't reconsider. He leaves that day. The church they attend tries to contact him, but he will not speak to anyone. Her life is shattered into a million pieces. She never saw it coming. Her Christian friends and church surround her to help her along. All she can really do is just keep breathing. Even doing simple tasks, like getting the girls to school, drain her to her core.

When she attends church, people who she only knew in passing, hug her and express their condolences. She starts to think that maybe they look down on her. Vain imaginations usually stalk those in pain. She sees a couple hugging in the lobby, and waves of shame hit her as she is reminded of her loss. Over the first few months, her emotions evolve from shock to hurt and pain.

By month four, the support of the church and Christian friends starts to drop off, and she feels the weight of being a single mom. Her pain has now transitioned into anger, and anger is an emotion that comes with some power behind it. Finally, something she can use! And boy, does she. She harnesses that emotion and uses it to stand up. You wouldn't call it anger if you saw her. Actually, she looks healthy. She cut her hair, joined a gym, bought new clothes and got a hobby. All very healthy, so nobody notices that the make-over is being driven by a hidden rage. After the divorces is finalized, she begins dating again, and within the next few years, she meets a wonderful man and marries again.

She looks better than ever; she appears to have come out on the other side. But deep inside, she's never really at rest. When her new husband calls to say he is running late, she wonders if there's someone else. On double dates with friends from church, she is fun and pleasant; but on the drive home, she comments that the other couple look "too happy." She is bothered how other young women dress around her husband. She is suspicious of them all.

With high school graduation closing in, she begins to be more protective and demanding of her girls than ever before. Going away to college is the next step in their journey, and on some subconscious level, it triggers a feeling that she is being abandoned all over again. Instead of discussing this with her husband, girls, friends, or Christian counselor, she turns to the one thing that saved her last time. Anger.

She has blow ups weekly with her daughters and finds fault with every friend and activity they want to do. To those around her, she is starting to look like a jealous, over-bearing, judgmental, controlling woman. But she is really just damaged. She is still in so much pain, only she's unaware of it, and those around her sure didn't notice the progression over the years. Her default position used to be one of love and acceptance, but now it is of judgment.

You see, there are stories just like that in churches everywhere. In fact, that story is 100 percent true. I know that woman. She is okay now, by the way. After one daughter refused to talk to her for a year, she walked into a counselor's office where she was able to unpack it all.

The problem with mean, judgmental people is that they don't come with a list of the hurts stapled to their forehead. They look strong, opinionated, and angry. Most of us will never put in the time to see if we can break through their walls to find out where things went bad. We assume they have a hard heart and have always been that way. If we're talking honestly, I have different scales for people although the Bible clearly says not to. And I have one very special scale that is reserved for just my own sins. When a car cuts in front of me with no thought, I assume he is simply a jerk and poor driver. Probably from New York! However, when I cut a person off, it was because I didn't see them or I was in a hurry. You should cut me some slack. Maybe you were in my blind spot. Perhaps I really needed to get to the hospital because that's where I turn left onto Hudson Avenue to get to where my movie is playing.

I can judge the other guy because I don't know him, so I allow myself to assign him motives that justify my feelings about his entire character. Motives are funny things, aren't they? It is the driving force behind so much good and so much evil in the world.

When I see others' sin, it's easy for me to assume they are bad people. However, when I sin, I choose to understand it was really the environment around me that helped to cause it. After all, I have pressure: a rough marriage, kids that are rude and disrespectful, and my boss is a jack donkey. Many times, it really is the pressures of our life that nudge us toward some pretty bad ideas. It's not an excuse for doing bad things, but it is fair to say that the grind of life (over thousands of days) leads us right up to the wrong doors. And that hallway has claimed more than a few of us.

It's also easy to assign better motives for the people we care about. Years ago, I served as a volunteer chaplain to youth that were imprisoned. The crimes these young people committed were what we consider extreme, adult and the most dreadful you could think of. It was consistently shocking to read about the crimes these baby-faced, pint-sized kiddos perpetrated. But despite their undeniably horrendous acts, every weekend, their moms, dads, uncles, aunts, sisters, and brothers poured into the detention center to love on them.

Many would not be free for years, if ever, but the love and rationalizing never stopped. "My baby is such a good kid," they would plead. "He just got in with the wrong crowd and did a bad thing." It's easy to brush that comment off as a parent overcome with pain. But in most cases, they were spot on. Most of these children are really great people. Overall, their life was pretty normal . . . right up to the night everything went to hell. Now they are paying a price for what turned out to be really only a very brief moment in their existence.

Now look through the eyes of the victims. They can only see a teenage monster. My point is, depending on whose eyes you look through you might see a monster or someone's baby. And amazingly, they are both right.

Live long and hard enough, and you will come to understand that we all have that baby and that monster inside our hearts and minds. We have gifts from God He said He will never take away. We can use them to bring so much needed good into a dark world, or we can use them to serve only ourselves; with that, the world grows a little darker, a little more hopeless.But it all depends on the eyes you are looking through.

And thus, we come to the notion of Christianity that we will see things most clearly when we look at each other through the eyes of our Father. It's work to intentionally stop and look at the homeless lady through God's eyes. Or how about the mean co-worker who has decided that you are their enemy? But when we do that, we might be surprised at what we see. Ultimately, we will treat people to the level of value we choose to assign them. I believe the key to not being a judgmental person is to place a high value on every person you see. What and who we choose to see as valuable exposes the values we hold dear in our hearts.

Years ago, I used to work downtown in of one of the largest cities in America. I was an executive in a rather large company. Like most big cities, we had quite the homeless population. Each morning, I parked in our company's garage and walked one block to our building. My short journey took me past several homeless people who had plenty of time to see me coming. It was always the same three or four vagabonds every day. They were normally hogging the bus stop bench so no one else could sit.

One guy, in particular, had a total of four teeth and would ask me for money every day in the exact same way. "Mornin' chief, you spare a few bucks for a brotha down on his luck?"

When I first started, I carried around change just to give to him. But over time, I got tired of it and started telling him all I had was credit cards. It's funny, I couldn't just say "no" so I lied because I'm a jerk like that. My guess is that life would have been set on repeat mode like a scene from Groundhog Day, if not for one morning and a God ordained, untied shoe.

Just as I reached the sidewalk, I realized I needed to tie my shoe, so I knelt down and started tying. Now, I don't want to brag, but I'm pretty good at it; I can actually tie my shoe AND double knot it without looking. My position gave me the perfect view of the homeless on the bus stop bench and at what happened next.

A woman (who was not homeless) was there with her little girl. My guess is the girl was three at the most. While the lady was digging in her purse, her daughter was repeatedly jumping on and off the sidewalk . . . And then the bus came rushing up. Like most city buses, this was going insanely fast. With her mother distracted, the little girl jumped a jump that really should have been her last. The bus slammed on its brakes as suddenly she was snatched back from harm's way. I couldn't see who had saved the little girl, but by now, I and those around me, were running to their aid.

As I got close, I saw the mom hitting the four-toothed homeless guy. All she knew was some derelict was holding her baby. We intervened and tried to explain what really happened. She just snatched her baby up and got on the bus. Everyone else went about their business, but I stood there stunned. This man just saved a kid's life. He returned to his place on the bench, turned to me and asked, "Hey chief, you spare a couple bucks for a brotha down on his luck?" "Yeah, I think I can do that."

You see, he now had value . . . at least to me. Not one day did he ever have to ask me for money again. I made a lot, so it was no hardship to give him cash. Those of us who saw it happen started telling the story to those we worked with. It wasn't long before we started seeing him in new shoes, jacket, and headphones. And then one day he was gone.

A wealthy, local restaurant owner took an interest in him, and just took him home one day. I was told he had paid to put him in a program to get him clean. He even paid for his dentures. I never saw him out there again, all because word got out about the value he had as a human being. It was a value he possessed all along.

Maybe it's hard for you to not find fault in others. Maybe you're not some mean, bad person but just one who still carries wounds that you can no longer see, but which cause you to act in ways you hate. I would encourage you to get counsel. Maybe you have been the victim of a judgmental feeding frenzy. I know it's hard, but you're going to have to forgive. If you don't, then the cycle could continue within you.

And then there's those of you who are very strong, and you don't really get moved when judgmental people criticize your life, actions, and motives. You should know that strength like that is a gift from God. You, my friends, are strong enough to storm their walls and find out what made them that way. You could rescue them from a life of hate, and you could stop them from damaging other people. Happy hunting.

Many U.S. cities have passed laws to make the homeless so uncomfortable they choose to move on. Laws like:

-The Sit-Lie Law, basically making resting in public areas illegal

-Making it illegal to give the homeless food

-Anti-panhandling laws which fine citizens if they are caught giving the homeless money

Appetizers

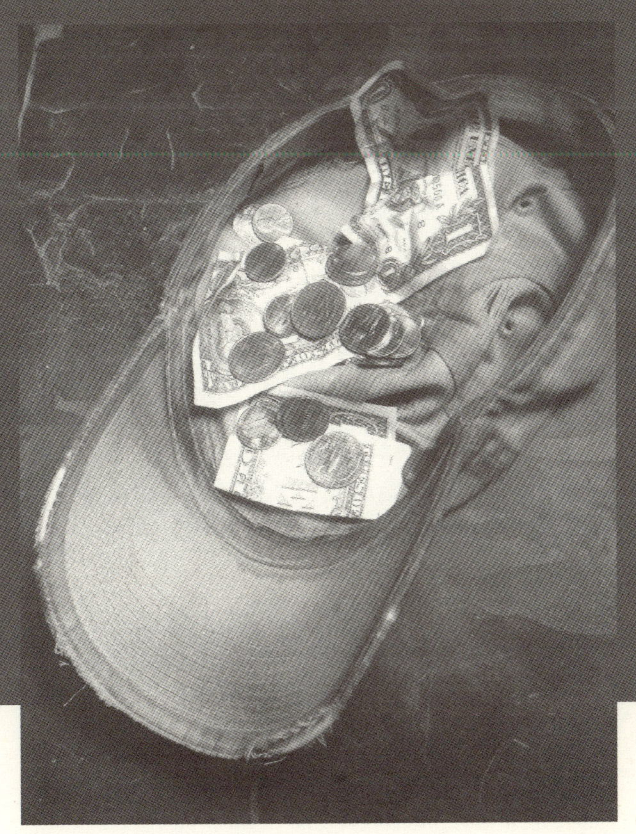

The best decision you can make is to follow Jesus, even when it goes against Christianity.

#WhyWeEatOurOwn

#why we eat our own 5

What Really Sank the Titanic

"We're one but we're not the same,
Well we hurt each other, then we do it again,
You say love is a temple, love a higher law,
Love is a temple, love the higher law,
You ask me to enter
but then you make me crawl,
And I can't be holdin' on to what you got,
When all you got is hurt"
U2 - One

My wife loves girl movies. It's a fact I've had to accept. Oh sure, I tried to change her during the first years of marriage, but you can only hypnotize a woman so many times before you're concerned about damage it may do to her later in life. So, I take my lumps like the defeated man I am. One of her all time favorite movies is Titanic. Spoiler alert: it sinks. Honestly, I really enjoyed it the first time I watched it. However, as of to date, I have watched that boat sink well over 300 times. I sit through Rose telling Jack that she will never let him go, as they float on the icy ocean. Very heartfelt. Of course, once Jack is a frozen buoy, she finds a whistle, is rescued, and moves on in life. I love that scene. I love it because it is the last scene in the movie, and when it's over, I am allowed to get up and move on with my life as well.

Now, although the entire movie drags for me, one part always pulls me in. It's in the first ten minutes when the researchers use a computer-generated image to analyze why the ship actually sank. You see, the Titanic was made with brittle steel and had some issues with the water-tight compartments that actually worked to help sink the ship faster than if it didn't have them at all. Add to that the fact they had removed many life boats because it was said the required amount made the ship look cluttered. With very poor visibility and one prideful captain who wanted to break records in arriving early, it stands to reason that someday James Cameron would make a movie about what happens next.

Odds are, no one who boarded the big and

powerful ship thought it would have an issue staying afloat. After all, one man was quoted saying, "Not even God Himself could sink this ship." Often, the seeds of disaster are planted in earlier dark years. In this case, they were built right into the interior steel of the ship, the management of White Star, and the heart of its leader.

Somehow, even today, we tend to equate size with stability. But the Scripture clearly teaches us that every work place, every house, every relationship gets tested. Life will indeed expose the cracks in all our lives. When these cracks are exposed, there are normally only two choices: some choose to cave in and give up, but there are those who decide to strengthen themselves in the broken places. I'm guessing it has always been this way.

Now, let's look briefly at some areas that are sinking our community of faith. Perhaps some of us will choose to work hard to fill in the cracks that seem to be spreading. Maybe you believe everything is fine. If you can't see that the American Church is having trouble staying afloat and relevant in today's world, then allow me to be the first to give you the red pill and welcome you out of the Matrix and into the stark reality our churches are in. Sure, there are exceptions, but they are just that - exceptions.

Plato once said, "The part can never be well unless the whole is well."

I couldn't agree more. We must begin to understand we are all in this together. Overall, many churches are in a fight to simply exist. Christ is becoming less important in our Western culture every year. Google this topic and read the studies. Involvement in churches is way down, as is attendance, giving, and the belief that church is relevant. I've heard key pastors and leaders blame this trend on declining moral behavior, the Internet, iPods, video games, and the selfishness of young adults. Sounds great to me because then I don't have to take any of the blame as a religious leader. "It's the world, God. They just don't care." Unfortunately, there are some other trends that fly in the face of this argument . . . pesky little things, like facts.

First fact is that although our churches are missing the 20 and 30 year-old crowds, overall, volunteerism within that age group is actually climbing in this country. They are all about causes. They buy products that promote fair wages in obscure countries, and many of them live on less so they can help build wells in Africa. No, I'm sorry. They aren't selfish. They just needed a better cause than raising money to recarpet the foyer. Blaming them for the Church's issue is as logical as blaming the Amish for global warming. So what's up, guys? Let's try something different. Let's hold ourselves personally responsible. It may not be our fault, but it is certainly our responsibility.

That's such a great word. Responsibility. If you break it down, it basically means "able to respond." You see, when I choose to take responsibility then I'm no longer a spectator; I'm a player. I believe we have to return to a few basic Biblical principles about building a church. Let's look for a moment at the icebergs that have become normal in today's church culture.

Gossip

Now, don't discount this! Please hear me out. Too many times we are looking for more advanced solutions to fix our churches. But, what if the fix is to return to the kindergarten lessons Jesus consistently taught. Gossip isn't sexy, but it has real teeth. It's true that you really only hear about it preached in youth groups. However, there is nothing childish about the damage it can cause.

Gossip doesn't stop when we grow up. As we mature, we learn gossip in a more clever way. Some of us could compete at an Olympic level. What a destructive habit! It's hard to know all the reasons people traffic in this. My best guess is that information is seen as position. If I know more than you and I'm passing information "down" to you, I am above you.

We need to return to the habit of stopping Christians midsentence when they begin to gossip. I promise you this will be very awkward. I promise they will start to gossip about you. But I also promise that if enough of us do this, the gossiper will start to become gun-shy before they even think to open their mouths. In my experience, when Christians stop and think before they speak, everyone wins.

Unforgiveness

During the last few years, I have been invited on numerous occasions, to help church leadership teams through difficult times or transitions. Many times, there were underlying offenses within the staff that worked against any vision or sense of camaraderie.

When I drag those issues out in the open, people tend to get a little weird and begin to speak like Christian lawyers. Normally, someone will argue this is not the appropriate setting to discuss a private matter between two people. Oh, come on! We are not going to change church culture by being appropriate. In fact, we need to be less appropriate and more authentic. And just so you know, if you and another person are at odds and everyone in the room can pick up on it, then you obviously had enough time to work things out on your own.

The Bible says we should be peacemakers, and

some peace comes only on the other side of war. So let the emotions out already! Inevitably, Christians will start speaking Christianese. We say very spiritual things that are pretty dumb. My personal favorite is when, in counseling, an argument breaks out and I step in and point out that they must really hate each other. "Whoa! That's a strong word," they retort. I ask what word they would assign to this feeling, and here is the reply I almost always get: "Well, I wouldn't say I hate (insert name here), but I just don't like 'em."

I would bet most of you have heard that phrase, haven't you? I would even bet most of us have even used it. I know I have . . . right up to the point I realized that it made absolutely no sense! I'm sure some will disagree with me, but in our Christian circles, we throw the word "love" around so much it means a thousand different things and rarely the real thing. Also, when did "like" become the power word?

Can you remember the first time you risked telling someone you loved them? It's a pretty big idea to throw out there. And then there is the moment we see if that person returns the same sentiment. If you hear, "I love you too," it's game on! But if they say, "Awww, thank you," or "I really like you, too." Then, as the kids say these days, "That's Jenga!" Game over.

You see, like comes with love. We can have

moments where we don't get along, but when the chips are down, love will give you away. I was once counseling a friend about how he felt very little emotion for his wife. They had been married 10 years, and he felt it had run its course. Ironically, during the meeting, he got a call that she had just been in an accident at work and was in an ambulance headed to the ER. We rushed out the door so he could be by her side. Her injury was severe, but she recovered. You see it? Love betrayed him. He later told me the thought of losing her snapped him back to what he really felt. Love betrays us in wonderful ways.

OK. Back to our meeting with the two team members who are sideways with one another. When all the positioning stops and we get on a level playing field, the truth comes out. Someone got offended and the offense began to fester. At first, both parties wanted to just let it go, but it never let go of them. Neither spoke about it, so it grew into an infection in the relationship which began to leak out onto the whole staff. A "staff" infection is bad news in any organization, especially in a church because people start to pick sides. And then the looks, shots, and passive-aggressive behavior start to fly.

It is at that moment that the enemy has us where he needs us. If he can keep us all fighting in the foxholes with each other, then his work is done. Once we recognize that we have let unforgiveness and bitterness in our life, we need to talk it out. This is not just true for people in ministry, but for all of us. Even if a person never wants peace, we need to force ourselves to press the reset button on our hearts so as not to keep score.

And the million dollar question is: "How do I learn to completely forgive?" Beats me. I still struggle with it often. One thing I do know is that you should be struggling with it. In the Christian culture, the phrase "I'm struggling with this" is most times translated "I'm still doing it." The word "struggle" implies a fight or a push.

In my experience, forgiving people is a continuous act. Just when I think I'm good with you, I might hear you say something that triggers waves of unforgiveness. But if you really apply yourself and fight the good fight, you can find yourself on the other side of this issue and genuinely love them. Some of the best friends I have to this day started out as people I felt I had to tolerate. I'm sure the feeling was mutual, but through the fight of forgiveness, we grew a little closer to the version of ourselves that God always wanted us to be. Keep struggling. You will be free.

Legalism

Cartoons really gave me a poor idea of what was

to come in my adult life. Back in my day, we didn't have a channel devoted 24/7 to cartoons. Instead, we only had Saturday mornings. As the sun rose on Saturday mornings, so did legions of kids all over America. Looking back on it now, I remember thinking that perils like quicksand and falling anvils were going to be a way bigger deal than they turned out to be. I mean, I have never once seen quicksand. I wouldn't even know where to find it if I wanted to. I never had to warn my friends enroute to my house, "Be careful coming down my driveway. Falling anvils happen from time to time." I wish cartoons would have given me hints about the real issues, like how to handle when your best friend wants to borrow money.

Perhaps, they could have spent a little more time teaching us about how to tell if an auto mechanic is robbing us blind. "Yes sir, I'm afraid we are going to have to replace the transmission because we found a hive of Keebler elves making meth in one of the wheel wells."

"Oh, okay. How much is that going to cost?"

"What does it matter?! Think of all the little elves who need saving! You have a moral responsibility!"

"Well then, of course! I want to support the health and well-being of the elfin youth."

Unfortunately, the warnings never came in

cartoons, so I was ill-prepared. Understanding the troubles ahead in life can really help you make course corrections. This is true in our everyday life, as well as when we come into the family of God. Personally, my early days of being a Christian were full of joy and passion. I was surrounded by such wonderful people who fed off the passion we newbies had for Christ. They were the ones who taught me how to study the Bible, how to pray, and how to hear and recognize the promptings from God. But they never thought to warn me about what a legalistic person could do to my faith. I was never given the signs to look for them when they showed up in my life. That was a lesson I was going to have to experience all on my own. And boy, did I!

It's a funny thing about a truly legalistic person: They rarely look legalistic. My first encounter was with a man in our church who seemed very kind and highly educated in the things of God. He had mastered the Scriptures like no one I knew. He could shape them into daggers and stab you in the face. He took an interest in me and began asking me questions that I was unsure how to answer. "You listen to secular music? You watched **that** movie? You went on a date with **that** girl? You didn't get up this morning and pray?"

With every question, I became more confused. I began to hear his voice in my ear when I did anything I enjoyed. I stopped dating that girl. I stopped watching movies outside of the Disney genre and turned my radio off for good. After about seven months of being mentored by this guy, I had successfully rid my life of all art, culture, and happiness. I was now a good Christian, but I was a miserable human being.

I began to mimic his behavior to my Christian friends. "You are going to see **that** movie?" "Can you please turn off **that** music while I'm in your car?" Slowly, I began to be excluded from social events because, quite frankly, I was a drag. Who knows how long I would have lived in that prison if it hadn't been for me walking into church early one day.

While sitting over a cup of coffee with one of the elders, my self-appointed mentor came by and fired a series of questions at me. As usual, I answered them all. After he walked away, the elder asked what that was all about. I told him how he was helping me to be a good Christian. The more I told him, the more he laughed. Really hard.

He led me to his office and gave me a brief dissertation about what it means to follow Christ. He explained what my conscience was and how God uses that to guide me. He said that although the man was a good person, he was steeped in legalism. Then he told me something I will never forget. "Michael, never let anything or anyone stop you from following Christ for yourself, even if it makes you look like, to some, a bad Christian." Pow! I was free.

I realized that although there were things God wanted me to put down, I had also given up things He never asked me to. My little friend was less than happy with my decision to date that girl. I married her, by the way. He was not happy with my choice of music, my earrings, or tattoos. But he wasn't God, so I was okay with being my own man. Towards the end of my time there, I was told that if I continued down this road, I would end up making irrational decisions that would ultimately send my life in an entirely different direction. He was right about that. I felt a call to ministry and took off after that. Legalistic Christians have an uncanny ability to drag an entire church down if they are left unchecked. They can begin to spread a false teaching of dogma and duties that overwhelms the church body like the flu. Ever so subtle, we start to jump through the hoops they have set up and forget to run the race Christ has set for each one of us individually. If we get infected, we drift into a checklist of "do's" and "don'ts." We begin to speak legal mumbo jumbo. And the real telltale sign is that the joy of following Jesus fades away.

I have heard the endless arguments from the legalistic flag wavers that warn if we are too free, we will end up skipping church, backsliding, and ultimately sacrificing goats in dark alleys with a guy named Earl who only wears ponchos. Sweet. Or . . . maybe God will begin to rock our boat when we begin to drift off the path a little, well before Poncho Earl builds the altar. Sometimes, I think we make a lot of rules God never gave us because we need to be able to know who is in and who is out. Legalism stunts the growth of the church. Let a legalistic person loose and unchecked in a growing church full of new believers and watch as it all comes to a grinding halt. It's quite a challenge to convince a deeply legalistic person to relax and change. Believe me, I have tried more than my fair share. Most of the time, they truly are okay being that way. As a pastor, it's my job to protect my church from these people.

Those truly free in Christ will always be bolder than the judgmental.

I'm fine when they choose to grace another church with their presence. I know all too well the destructive power of law without relationship. You want to do an interesting personal study? Ask at least 10 Christians who have stopped attending church why they quit. You will be stunned at how many of them left because a legalistic person treated them poorly. Many go on to explain that they never got support from the leaders in dealing with it in any real way. Work as a Christian leader long enough, and you'll see that when legalistic Christians are not confronted by church leaders, this becomes one of the primary reasons people simply take their faith mobile.

The church of Jesus needs to become a growing faith again. I believe that things will, indeed, turn around because we have truth on our side. God absolutely loves every person and is not about to give up on this generation. When the youth find secular organizations asking them to lay down their lives and help others, they go. They long to be part of something radical and full of purpose. This sounds, to me, exactly like the way the Christian faith is supposed to be lived. We are to be the first ones in when natural disasters happen in our communities. We are to be the ones who take hills and bring a powerful vision worth dying for. We are to lead our generation. But where have we gone?

In the void that churches have left, some very passionate leaders have risen. I was talking to a 28-year-old man who recently came to Christ who said something eye opening. He said that he will always consider Bono, lead singer from the band U2, his first pastor. The young man went on to tell me it was Bono's call to prevent the spread and suffering of AIDS and the call to do more to help others around the world that pastored him. He heard Bono talk about how the Western world needed to get off their rears and do something. The famous shade-wearing rocker had challenged him. I couldn't help but agree. I love Bono and his music, but it's his heart that makes me continually give money to his causes. I like that he has a bold vision about forgiving debt in some third-world countries. Bono has played a vital role of caring for the world.

Maybe we could stop all the gossip, unforgiveness, and legalism and help him in caring for the world God actually asked the Church to care for. It's either that or we can keep singing "Row, Row, Row Your Boat" on the deck of our very own Titanic. Your call.

Appetizers

Between 1828 and 2007, an estimated 26 ships have sunk due to collisions with icebergs.

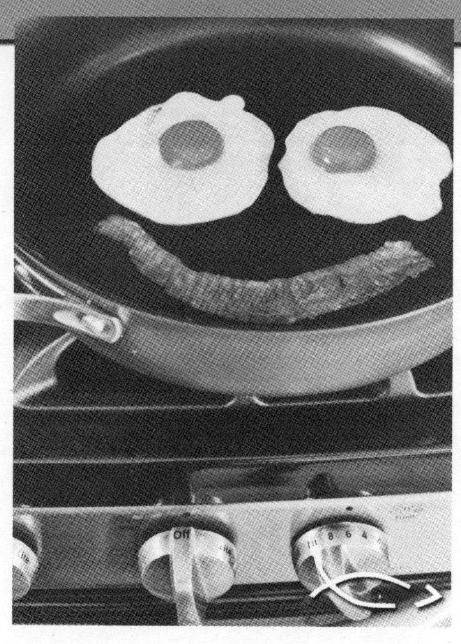

Everyone has a church:
a gym, bar, reading group,
social media or a religion.
God built community into our DNA.
#WhyWeEatOurOwn

#why we eat our own 6

Because I Won't See You Sunday

"But I'm on the outside, I'm looking in,
I can see through you, see your true colors,
'Cause inside you're ugly, you're ugly like me,
I can see through you, see to the real you"
Staind - Outside

I would like to talk to all my friends out there who have decided to leave the local church for the freedom of following God on your own. Don't panic. I just want to talk a little, okay? Think of me as the De-churched Whisperer for this chapter. I know you have been hurt and even misunderstood. I know you like being the wild stallions, frolicking in the fields of grace and free Sundays. Hey, I get it! Remember I was going to leave as well. I'm just gonna throw some grain out in the trough and leave the corral gate open. If you feel like it, come on in and nibble on some oats. Don't worry. I won't try to close the gate on you and try to break you. If I make any sudden movements, then you can jump the fence and be gone for good.

Okay, let me just share with you a few of my musings about what is happening to both those who have left and the rest of us who have stayed. First, I do agree with your position that you don't have to be part of a local church to be a Christian. After talking with so many of you, I can clearly see that you're still very much about your faith, and I really do respect your free will. I, for one, will never judge you if you never return to a local church. Many of us leading church have really begun to feel your hearts and what has led to this massive escape.

In many ways, what the church is going through feels like a divorce. When a family becomes fractured, not all the cracks surface instantly; some take a while. For those of us who are still in local churches, we have noticed some new cracks. And while we understand your feelings about why you left, maybe for a moment you could hear the heart of those who stayed. Let us share with you how we feel about all this.

We miss you. We miss the leadership you took with you. We miss the wisdom you brought to the table. We miss the gifts God gave you. We miss your hands and feet that worked tirelessly to help others. We miss your ability to question our bad habits. We miss your smiles. We miss being a family. It is true that you can be a Christian without us, but it is also true that we cannot be a whole body without you. We are going to limp through this generation and never live up to our entire potential if you never return. In short, you're missed.

There. That felt good to get all that out there. Now, let me share the last 10 percent with you as well. I personally think it's you guys that are going to turn the church around in this country. I'm just going to boldly hang it all out there.

I think leaving was a smart move. After all, you at least did something. Movement is so peaceful to us on a basic level. When my kids were babies and couldn't sleep, I would load them in the car and go for a drive in the middle of the night. It didn't take long and they were resting peacefully. But I didn't stay gone forever. Eventually, I had to come home. You, who had the courage to break away, hold the DNA of a leader. You hold the bias for action and change. You are not afraid of being seen as different or as a rebel. So now, come and help lead the rest of us "out of church" and back into our communities. Come show us how to talk about God in a real way without making it feel like a sales pitch. Show us how to laugh again. Help us to lose our fear of man and be the person God has called us to be.

You know in your heart that we can do so much more good together than apart. We don't have to get married. Let's date a while. Come see if it's a good fit. If some churches are unwilling to change and to grow in love and serving others, then avoid those. But churches are still full of people who think, feel, and believe just like you. We have been standing on the walls and keeping the torches burning for better days ahead. Many have been fighting for your place here.

We can be a city on a hill again. We can be hope to a fallen world. We can use our resources, time and energy to do more than remodel the church offices every other year. Let's meet tornadoes, floods, hurricanes, and fires with waves of support, care, love, and money. Let's do it better than anyone on earth. Let's show up as a fully functioning army for the battle for the hearts of people; armed with love, forgiveness, grace, strength, and humility. Yeah, let's try this all again.

Let's get involved in more social issues. Let's be friends again. Let's be broken together, because broken people have the ability to heal each other in ways the unbroken can never understand. I'm sure we will have our moments and get into a few fights, but we can work out our petty differences. Whenever I think about making peace with others, I always think of Good Times Adventures in Breckenridge, Colorado. And boy, does it live up to its name! Every year, my family, staff and I go there to ride snowmobiles and dogsleds. We really like snowmobiling all the way up to the Continental Divide. It's like seeing the Grand Canyon; it really lives up to the hype. Add to that the fact that the guides are quite possibly the funniest people on earth, and you can't help but have a blast. Not once have I gone that I haven't laughed hot chocolate right out of my nose.

Snowmobiling is fun, but our favorite thing to do is go dogsledding. I promise you, it is ten times more brutal than being on a snowmobile. Those dogs are not normal dogs. I don't want to start an investigation, but I think the dogs are on some kind of performance-enhancing drugs.

While we are inside suiting up in the warm and waterproof snowsuits provided, the dogs have already been attached to the sled and are waiting for us to meet them. We take a few minutes to learn their names and take pictures with them. Normally, this goes off without a hitch.

However, on my turn, two of the dogs paired side-by-side decided to fight. Now, I don't mean they got a little snippy . . . I mean full on "I'm going to kill you and wear you as a coat" fight. I did what every man should do and used my 15-year-old son to shield me from any possible attack. Look, I'm fine standing toe-to-toe with any person, but I don't do dogs. My son was fine, and after some more counseling and a few years of trust issues, I'm sure we will have a very pleasant relationship again. But the guide did something that seemed unwise. He stood over them and reached into the fight.

As they continued to fight, he knelt over them, held their heads together, placing them between his legs so that he was essentially sitting on them. I realize this is a Christian book, but let's be honest, if two dogs are trying to bite each other, there are two maybe three places you may want to keep them away from. As a man, I can tell you that he had them next to my ground zero. Amazingly, as soon as his weight was on them, they stopped biting. They still growled a little but with each jerk or growl, the guide stayed put until suddenly they were fine.

He got up, and they popped right up as well, looking around like nothing had happened. He petted them and they licked his face. Yuck! The guide apologized and explained that these two dogs didn't really like each other. I felt the need to share some leadership wisdom and suggested that maybe they should be positioned with different dogs so as not to get on each other's nerves, or even better, put them on different dogsledding teams altogether.

The guide explained that dogs are pack animals, and so there will always be one dominant leader. In this case, it had to be him. Dogs are very smart and would learn that if they fight, they would get their way, making a guide's job harder. "By forcing two fighting dogs together and sitting on them, I am asserting my dominance the way an alpha dog would. And by forcing them together, I am letting them know that this is what I want."

As a side note, this whole sitting on something to get dominance does not work on women, because my wife was less than impressed, and I actually got bit. But for dogs, they understood clearly that the leader had said, "You **will** work together," and after that, they seemed to behave the rest of the day. I'm starting to get the idea that as Christians, God is wanting to force those of us fighting to be together, and He is putting pressure on us to do things His way now. The longer we don't use our gifts or work in unison, we start to forget who we could have been.

I heard a story about Ronald Reagan towards the end of his life. As you may know, he was suffering from

Alzheimer's Disease, and so his memory was fading. One afternoon, he walked into the kitchen from his office. Nancy noticed that one of his arms was wet from the shoulder down, and he seemed to have something clinched in that hand. She asked, "What do you have there, Ronnie?" He held his hand open and said, "I don't know, but I think it has to do with me." In his hand, was a small replica of the White House that was made for his fish tank. He had reached in to retrieve it because somewhere deep inside, he knew that had to do with him.

In the same way, we may look at a hurt world and know we are supposed to be a part of fixing it, but we just can't remember how. The ball is in your court.

According to the Hartford Institute for Religion Research:

-The average church in the U.S. has 75 regular participants in worship on Sunday mornings.

-2011 was a record year for church foreclosures.

Appetizers

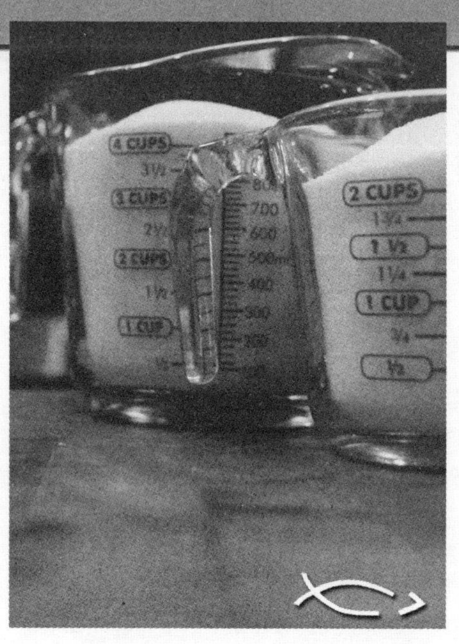

There are many things you can find in the heart of a successful person, but excuses is not one of them.

#WhyWeEatOurOwn

#why we eat our own 7

Fire House Accountability

"If I fall along the way,
Pick me up and dust me off,
And if I get too tired to make it,
Be my breath so I can walk"
Matchbox Twenty - Bent

I wasn't around Christians very long before I became well acquainted with the word "accountability." Mostly, the phrase that was thrown around quite a bit was "accountable TO . . ." Funny how much it is used considering it appears in the Bible only a few times. Honestly, I began to have less respect for that word when I saw how it was put into use.

When I was younger, I attended an "accountability group" for a while. It was made up of several unmarried men in their early twenties who wanted to stay accountable to each other for things men struggle with. That's a softball way to say we were supposed to stop each other from watching porn, having sex, getting drunk, or doing anything that seemed sinful. And just to be very clear, it didn't work at all. Sure, it all sounded great, but it quickly became apparent that accountability wouldn't do for our behavior what our character and morals were supposed to do. Each week, we would meet for an hour or so and confess our bad thoughts and deeds. Every week, some of us would do good and some not so good. But for one young guy, every week was an epic fail. He had developed a bad habit of looking at porn at a very young age, as well as some drug addictions, so he was just a real mess.

As the year went on, several of the guys got more and more frustrated with him. They would accuse him of not even trying or not loving God enough to change. Each time he would have tears and say sorry, but it seemed as if he would never overcome. It all came to a head one day when I was asked to come to the group an hour early so we could discuss something. When I showed up, the only guy not invited to that secret meeting was our struggling friend. During our discussion, I realized we had been brought in before him so we could all agree to ask him to leave our accountability group. The reasons seemed logical. They threw around Scriptures about knowing people by their fruit and such. I listened and agreed that he really didn't fit. After all, if he wasn't going to even try, then he shouldn't be with those of us who are trying to become better Christians. When he arrived, we broke the news to him. There was some drama and emotions about it, but overall, he was very understanding. He left that day and never came back to the group. At least, I think that's what happened. I never went back either. Of course, my reasons were different.

You see, I never went back because, unlike him, I had never been truthful to those guys anyway. I was sleeping with my girlfriend and wouldn't tell them because they knew her, her family, and all her friends. I justified it because I loved her and we were going to get married . . . and we did. But that group was, to me, a nice attempt at a bunch of great ideas failing in very fallen young men.

Even for those who did admit failing in an area, there wasn't anything we could do or say that really left an impact. Should we lecture them, tell them to pray harder or just slap them? No, we all just listened and said to keep trying. After that whole experience, I really hated hearing the word "accountability" thrown around in church leadership situations.

Many times, it was used by the older leaders to control the younger staff. They were letting them know who was in charge or how they could be punished if their behavior displeased those they were accountable to. Accountability began to be used as a tool to manipulate people into being quiet and not questioning things we did not really agree with or understand.

An odd truth is that accountability seems all fine and dandy, but for many, it lacks real depth to hold us with any force of conviction. It's only useful if we have some skin in the game. For example, if I say something rude to a clerk I don't know at a store I rarely go to, I can move on and not care at all. However, if I say those same rude words to my wife or a friend, I am eventually forced to deal with it because of my proximity to them on a daily basis. And there can be even more forces pushing me in accountability because I genuinely do care about their feelings and how they think of me. That poor clerk I'm rude to in the store is out of sight, so out of my character-care zone. "Oh well, sorry, God. I'll do better next time." Another routine scenario is that if I'm accountable to you and we both struggle with the same sin we can drift into simply having a "secret club" about our struggles. And then there are the issues that come if I don't struggle with what you're fighting against, I can simply listen, not really understand and say things like, "I'll pray for you."

Now, please understand those were just my experiences. I'm sure many have had great success with accountability, but through many conversations in researching this topic, I have found numerous stories of people who have had very similar outcomes. I honestly think I would have just stayed with my disdain for that word if it hadn't been for the several years I spent as a professional firefighter. During my first year of training, they used the word accountable often but in a radically different way. They too added a little word at the end, but it wasn't "accountable to" but rather "accountable for." We were accountable FOR each other. It was a complete paradigm shift for me in more ways than just firefighting.

You see, when we are in a burning building, firefighters are paired up. We are both responsible to get our partner through this fire or emergency and return him back home, intact, to his family, friends, and his life when the shift at the firehouse is over. It doesn't matter if your partner made a mistake or a bad judgment call that got him in trouble. You're accountable FOR him. Period. Get him out of danger. Don't even think about leaving him behind! No excuses, no giving up, no blame, and certainly no whining. Sure, chew him out later if he made a stupid move, but right now

. . . "We are getting you out of here, my friend!"

When you are accountable FOR another, you cannot ask them to leave a group. You don't get to call a timeout in the middle of life's storms. You have to help them even if it hurts you. And if it comes to it, you trade your life for theirs. You may get on each other's case later, but friendship at that level can always work through conflict. We don't leave our partners. EVER. Firefighters use little catch phrases like, "If you go, then we both go." And, "Everyone goes home today." They have a keen sense of awareness that the stakes of their job are incredibly high. Firefighters traffic in human suffering. That is also very true for the men and women who serve in all types of ministry. Being a firefighter changed my entire outlook about how I apply accountability in church work. The word now brings me comfort and security instead of being a punchline in a joke.

When outlining our core values at the church I pastor, one of the core values is that we are all accountable FOR each other. If one of us falls, we are not going to kick them out of the club, staff, or church. We are going to stay with each other until we clear the danger. If a staff member falls, they don't just lose their job or position. They get to be helped back up on their feet. We believe our mistakes can be just as big of "God moments" as the successes in our life. Accountability in my life means I can share the worst parts of my character with my staff and fellow leaders, and in turn, they can share theirs with me. No one gets left behind. No one lives under the cloud of their failure forever on this team.

Over the years, we have had it tested a few times. One such time, a young staff member got into some sin that was rather hurtful to his reputation and a relationship. Several people in the church found out about it and demanded that he be fired. We all stood together and said, "No way! If he goes, we all go." We met with the disgruntled church members and clearly communicated to them in very colorful and vivid terms that they would lose all of the leaders if they ran this guy off. Our worship leader, support staff, all our youth pastors and every other staff member said they would all quit; they would not be part of a church that needed perfect leaders. I explained that we could pack up and go start a church anywhere. And you know what? Most backed off. A few left, but who cares. They obviously don't understand the power of love, friendship, forgiveness and loyalty. The moral mistake had happened, and he owned it. He worked to heal the ones he hurt, and that chapter is over in his life.

That happened so long ago that we never even

think about it, and the young man who had a momentary failure has become a trusted key leader here now. He came out of it better for some strange reason we can't understand. Only God can make all things work for His glory. And so He does.

At some point, I just think that the church has got to be a church for the leaders too. They deserve some protection and healing as much as the average person in the seats. Maybe, at times, they need even more. This kind of accountability doesn't appeal to some. I get emails about how this is a wrong way to live or build a team. Maybe. I guess we will all find out over the course of our lives because everything gets tested.

So far, however, it has been a pretty messy way to live, but at the same time it gives us all a very secure feeling that we can be open with each other. People can walk away from our team or our church because that's their choice. However, if they choose to stay and do life, ministry and community with us, then we are all accountable for each other. We are accountable to get through our lives and callings until we all get home. No excuses, no giving up, no blame, and certainly no whining.

JOURNEY
FIRE
SCIENCE
FIRE DEPT

Appetizers

One of the most common mottos for fire departments in the U.S. is: "Everyone goes home." It's a statement that embodies their core belief that they will all work together to get each man or woman back to their family at the end of their shift.

The church must be about grace.
We forgive, we heal, we restore, and we repeat.
Bank on it, that's how churches grow.
#WhyWeEatOurOwn

#why we eat our own 8

Church Fight Club

A come-to-Jesus meeting for all of us who have already come to Jesus

"Just gonna stand there and watch me burn,
Well that's alright because
I like the way it hurts,
Just gonna stand there and hear me cry,
Well that's alright because
I love the way you lie,
I love the way you lie"
Eminem, Rihanna – Love The Way You Lie

Let me tell you an awkward thing I have found about being an author. In preparing for releasing this, my second book, I sent it to several church leaders and authors I really respect. I asked them for their thoughts and would they consider endorsing it. Everyone I asked was willing to give me a "shout out," as the kids say these days. But more than a few said. "Just write something for me, and I'll sign it." Uhhh? Okay? What a nightmare!

I tried but ultimately just gave up because it just sounded too stupid. I mean, think about it for a second. I can't be too extreme with another's voice or feeling about my work; I might go too far and will look like a jerk to them: "Michael is so wonderful and gifted at writing that sharks actually have a week dedicated to him." Signed, some great church leader. And if I am too self-abasing with my own work, then no one will want to read it. "Michael's writing is okay-ish and he says some truth, some funny things and then leaves space in the margins for you to color in if you get bored." Yikes! I hate that. Many well-known authors have told me this practice is pretty common place, but I just can't do it.

If I'm making statements for famous people about my work, then why not swing for the fences? "Michael's writing is the greatest thing I have read on the Internet." Signed, Abraham Lincoln. That should really lock down some purchase power.

The simple truth is that when we step up and speak for another, there is always the risk that you might not communicate it the way they would. But when a person or people group cannot speak for themselves, then I believe you must put risk aside and begin to communicate. That is what this chapter is. I'm going to talk for a group of people who, most of the time, cannot say the things in their heart. It's actually quite ironic because they are the most gifted communicators you will ever meet. They are your church pastors and ministry leaders.

Now, in unpacking why Christians can be so vicious to each other, pastors and church leaders have to take their fair share of the fault. After all, we are the leaders, and so we can't simply shrug off the fact that we are accountable for the things we tolerate. The church leaders I know all have stories of things they handled wrong and how it damaged someone. If you ever find a church leader who says they have never mishandled a person or situation, then my advice is to back away slowly and get away from them. I know I have caused more than my fair share of damage because I thought I knew what I was doing. Many times, I have erred on the side of expedience over grace.

The problem with being a pastor or church leader is that you cannot be trained in a controlled environment or with robots. We work with real people, with real issues, real marriage problems, and real pain. And it all comes at us at once. You're crazy if you think we are not going to make some poor decisions. And with every poor decision, we can cause pain.

But we are not the only ones who cause pain. We are just the ones who cannot say anything about it. You see, in church work, we get complaints in real time. Every week our churches receive emails and calls from church members upset about something or someone. We listen and try to address each one as soon as it's on our radar. Most of the time, they are just going through a rough time and getting a little too amped up. But if a church leader begins to feel negativity towards you or the church body, in general, what do they do with that? Tell you? No way! That could have real consequences!

This is how some ministry leaders become hostages to the people they really love and serve. When relationships become too one-sided, they often come to an end. For many church leaders, it becomes less a profession and more like an abusive relationship. According to the churchconference.com, scbaptist.org and news-journal.com, 1,500 pastors leave the ministry each month. I'm not making up this statistic. Maybe if Christians knew how some of them felt deep down, then perhaps a few mature and loving people in the church would begin to look out for the ones who live to look out for you.

So just for a moment, allow me to stand up for some of my brothers and sisters in our profession. First, I'm going to share some widely-held, hidden feelings. Then I'll share some practices that have been put into place within the churches I partner with that turned out to be life and career saving for the staff. For speed sake, I'm going to use the word "we" a lot. I'm also going to group all ministry leaders and pastors together. I know it's risky, but some of this will never be said if we don't just let it fly.

It's going to hurt, and you won't want to believe some of the truths about your leaders. But know that even if they won't openly admit to it, there will be truth in what I am about to say. Much of it will offend you because it needs to. It doesn't make it less true. A few of the words I choose may make you pull back. Don't. Push through, all the way, so we can get to the core.

All right, time to unpack the hard stuff. Sometimes ministry leaders hate the people they lead. Yes, hate. Maybe not you specifically, but the idea of you, the idea of another church member making another demand. It is absolutely a sin when leaders do it (hate), but it is also absolutely happening. Sure, most of them wouldn't use the word hate because they have been trained to edit things to a softer, more acceptable word. But the word hate is in the Bible, and we are told that men and woman will, at times, struggle with it. So why not just own it if it fits?

Hate is defined as "intense hostility and aversion usually derived from fear, anger or sense of injury." Sometimes the men and women who lead churches get shoved in a corner by the very people they lead. The demands put on our ministry teams are never fully understood by the average attender because the bulk of what leaders do must be kept private. Our leaders are vastly outnumbered, and most churches are incredibly understaffed.

Each week, they are required to make money stretch further than what's possible, help marriages be restored, care about the youth, plan services, make calls, return emails, and about a hundred other duties. Add to that any drop by(s) or emergencies that come up within the church. That's a tall order! Don't forget the fact that most of our leaders have families and children who they want to spend time with and a God they should talk to from time to time since they work for Him.

For many leaders, it's just impossible to fit it all in, so they are left with decisions as to what doesn't make the cut. Too often, it is their families and time with God. All of that can really take a toll. It's not hard to understand how some leaders just begin to feel like the rules of ministry are a no-win situation. It's like if someone was to remove your lungs and then demand that you breathe.

Sometimes the emotion of it all simply brings leaders to a place of anger, resentment, and finally hate. Allow me to recap a few things I said earlier in the book about what is acceptable for the average church attendee and what is acceptable in the life of a ministry leader. Christian leaders are well aware that almost every piece of information that gets out about them, their family, their hobbies or even social interactions will have the potential to irritate someone in the congregation. Leaders live with an awareness that church members might choose to use that information to get offended and, in turn, leave the church.

I know several pastors who drive to another town to see movies that might cause issues with some of their people. Church leaders are often judged on what music they listen to, what other pastors they quote, who they are friends with, what they spend their money on, if they get tattoos, if their kids get tattoos. They can offend people if they drink alcohol while, at the same time, offend others if they choose not to drink. Many leaders within our churches get questioned about how they let their children dress, what age they let them date and even who they allow their kids to date. The list could go on for quite a while. Talk about living in a fish bowl!

You see, every one of those decisions comes with a few people who might be upset; and for some, these may be deal breakers for them to continue attending that church. And yes, there are a lot of Christians that can be that catty and small-minded. But if enough of them leave, how will the church survive?

So we set up board of directors, committees and overseers to define acceptable behavior for pastors and church leaders. Sometimes, instead of protecting their leaders, who only want some semblance of normalcy, the boards choose to protect the finances of the church. That means their pastors need to keep butts in the seats and the offerings up. That can't happen if people leave.

Instead of having the courage to stand up to manipulation and control, some boards and committees have chosen to release a leader from their church in order to keep the giver happy and committed. And if a leader does something really wrong, justice is swift and without grace. Things of this nature always prompt me to play the "What If?" game. I want to cover something I have said a few times, but I would like to do it a different way. I want to be able to stop the story and change factors as a kind of an experiment. This may seem repetitive, but this point needs to be driven home. Humor me a minute, and think of a typical pastor who falls into sin and is found out. Let's say he was the founding pastor, and the church runs 700 people weekly. Let's all agree that the normal things would probably happen:

He is fired instantly and asked to go sell cars or something while he goes through a "restorative process." That phrase is Christian leader code for "fix your marriage and lie to yourself that we will let you lead here again." If our recent church history has taught us anything, it's that this process will not lead to any kind of restoration, but rather it will give the church leaders enough distance and time to overcome the congregation's love and desire to help their friend, pastor and his entire family. In all honesty, we actually try to create a long-distance relationship between a fallen leader and his church. We do this because we all know that long-distance relationships rarely work. On some mean and cruel level, it's actually pretty smart.

Now, he and his wife are alone - asked to not come back to that church because it would be to awkward. So, they look for another church. Surprisingly, they find a kind and wonderful church that welcomes them in, but alas, it just feels "off." They want to go home and be with the people that they built their life with, but the leaders of the church have asked them not to. In fact, it was written into the contract they signed in order to receive a severance pay. A year or so passes, and they finish all the counseling. Things are better than ever in that pastor's marriage. They ask to come back now but again are asked not to because "The new pastor needs to be free from this drama so he can heal the church." And round and round it goes in communities all over this nation.

But what if? What if we change the pieces around just for fun? What if we get very honest with our values and driving influences in our churches? Let's be brutally honest okay? No cheating. Ready?

What if this pastor who had built this church and had this moral failure was actually the biggest giver to the church financially? Let's say he inherited $500 million because his father was an oil tycoon. Let's say he never had taken a salary, and this church was able to employ way more staff and do way more ministries than a church 10 times the size. Without his giving, 30 staff member may lose their jobs.

Do we think that the whole thing would have been handled exactly the same? Do you think that pastor and his wife would have been asked to take their attendance and giving to another church? Do we think maybe the church leaders might have thought about navigating this differently so he and his wife were still somehow part of this body even if he wasn't leading?

Think about it, Church. Think about it, elders. Think about it, committees, overseers and board members. We all know, deep down, in places we won't talk about that if that was the case, there is no way on earth it would be handled the same way. We tend to place a higher value on money than on people and their giftedness. And it actually happens in some churches everyday.

When a person with money who gives a lot to the church fails (has an affair or an addiction), the support can often be way bigger than when a person of lesser influence falls. Just look at who ends up getting the church in a divorce. I have actually seen a church support the husband, who had the moral failure, and asked his ex-wife to leave because it would be "weird" if she stayed. The reason? He made the big bucks and gave generously.

Not every church is guilty of this, but there is enough of it going on that we are all going to have to take the heat for this slide in our moral compass. Too many times in our American churches, money makes the rules. I don't even believe it's because we are greedy. I think it's because we are afraid. And money may not buy happiness but it sure can rent security and stability.

Yep, it's a tough job being a ministry leader when you have to serve God and money. But often those big issues are only the tip of the iceberg of what consistently comes at leaders. Allow me to share some kind of everyday annoyances that help to wear out our local church leaders.

Some pastors get handed books every week on how churches should be run. Often, this can be a passive-aggressive way of forcing a leader to do things in a different way. Many will even stalk the pastor for a book report for the next few months. Please stop giving them those books! Most have just enough time to read the ones they want to read.

Ministry leaders sometimes get lectures from some well-meaning, wealthy people in their church advising them to take a vacation at such and such a place because it will be good for them and their family, not really understanding that they just can't afford that kind of trip.

Church leaders often get pressured to promote someone's business in the church. It is spun like a money-making opportunity for the church in that business generated will result in a percentage donated to the church. Why can't they just build their own business and donate a percent of that to the church? In total disclosure, leaders know some people only attend their churches to make business connections. They don't care, but people who attend church for that reason should know that leaders know.

Other church members think they have an idea for a great fundraiser. Listen, just because a Christian thinks an idea for raising funds is great does not mean it is actually a great idea at all. If leaders have to plan, staff, fund and execute a month-long fundraiser that will ultimately bring in a grand total of $84 for the Youth Department, then many leaders are going to pass. Just because a church leader may not love an idea doesn't mean they don't love the person who brought it up. Yes, even wonderful, well-meaning Christians can put undo strain on a staff's time and resources without even knowing it.

Some Christians demand to get counsel only from the main pastor while there are several other staff members who are just as capable. Odds are they are going to tell them the exact same thing anyway.

There is also a group of Christians who rarely come to an actual church service and yet stop by church offices each week so the minister can counsel them about life issues. They need to understand that when people teach on Sunday mornings, it's really a giant counseling session anyway, and the weekly visits are draining leaders with their need for their own private services.

I'm sure some of your heads are spinning a bit because there is a lot of new truth packed in here. However, I promise you that it is spot-on accurate. I know these things all too well because, in addition to having experienced them myself, I have a lot of ministry friends and these are the things we talk about when all the church members have been tucked in. You ever notice when a visiting pastor comes into town, often your pastors or leaders will go out and eat and not invite anyone from the church to join them? Many times it's so they can share frustrations like these with each other and not feel so alone.

Sometimes the thought of having to make one more call, sit through one more marriage counseling session, or answer one more angry email makes us feel trapped, cornered, spent and used. That's when anger shows up. He brings with him emotions very normal for an exhausted person. Spiritual leaders have emotions and breaking points like everyone else.

Christians freak out when people in ministry are caught in sin because they were supposed to be above reproach. Right? Christians make comments like: "They must have had a secret life." No kidding!

That's all they had! Church leaders can spend their adult lives learning how to hide things from everyone, then suddenly we forget where we hid our happiness, joy, fulfillments, and, oh yes, our calling. And just like when we go searching for our keys when they're lost, we can find things we weren't even looking for. And sometimes hurting lost leaders find the wrong thing.

The body of Christ needs to wrap its mind around the fact that if the hemorrhaging of leaders away from the church doesn't stop, things are going to get even worse. The Church will not get what it deserves. She won't get what she wants or even what she pays for. She will not get what she loves. People. If we don't start showing real love to the people serving in our churches then they will find a more loving place to go.

I've had too many friends who have already left ministry for the marketplace because they feel much more love and purpose in those places than in church. I personally know gifted guys and gals who went to Google and Apple. Several moved to Nashville and California to be studio musicians. I know five senior pastors who left their churches for sales jobs in industries like medical and pharmaceutical sales. I know people who left ministry and opened coffee shops, daycares, tutoring centers and adventure outfits. One went back to school to get a Psychology degree. In every case, these were not lazy paycheck players in the church. On the contrary, they were some of the best in what they did in the church. They just didn't want the church politics and junk that came with being in ministry any longer. But here is a sobering wakeup call . . . They didn't leave their calling, just the church. If you look closer at the leaders who have left, they almost all landed in a job they love, doing something close to what they felt called to in the church.

Christians as a whole lost some great tech and media people. We all lost gifted musicians, worship leaders and an awesome counselor. The youth pastor runs an adventure company now, the children's ministry pastor and his wife opened a daycare, and other pastors are using their considerable skills to sell things. We lose our most gifted and ground-breaking leaders because the world and marketplace show them more value, forgiveness and even freedom than we did.

And just so we are clear on this . . . gifting matters. We need to dispel the thinking many Christians have that any ol' person can fill leadership roles in church. I'm surprised how many times I have heard wonderful Christians denigrate what it takes to be an effective leader in the body of Christ. Many times, Christians treat their leaders in the church like they don't have real jobs. After all, working at a church must be like living in Candy Land.

It's exactly that misguided attitude that gets passed around until everyone who is dissatisfied with their job thinks they could go lead a church, ministry, be a counselor, or missionary. Let me be blunt. Every position in ministry requires tools and skills that make a person fit well. If you don't like people and can't keep a secret, then you're not going to be a good counselor. It doesn't matter how good a listener your girlfriend says you are. Just because some people make ministry leadership look easy, don't be fooled; it demands talent, courage, and problem-solving skills that not everyone possesses.

Yes, it's going to be rough the next 20 years watching our greatest leaders break records and bring innovation to the business world while we are left with leaders who will serve because no one else wanted the job.

If this all sounds harsh, I understand, but we are sinking so fast that we have lost the time to dance around these issues and pretend we are going to be saved by some kind of angel in the outfield moment.

No, we are going to need to change our church culture. We are going to need to go back to letting our budget be defined by the vision God has given us instead of letting the budget decide God's ability to direct where we go, what we build, who we reach, and who gets forgiveness.

We are going to have to let the men and woman in our churches take risks without making them run it through a board of men so far out of understanding culture they think Kanye West is an airline.

We need to let our gifted woman lead as well. Many churches have really started getting better at this, but there are some who think they can't be used and that is cutting the potential pool of leaders in half.

Churches need to plan today for the storms that can and will come whether we want them or not. What will your church do if a key leader has a moral failure? If they sincerely repent, are you willing to stick with them?

In our church, we won't fire them if they say "sorry" and work to fix the problem. It has been tested once and survived fine. It wasn't a massive thing, but we held to our belief and our church grew stronger. We drill it in every year that our leaders are not only human but also awesome.

Senior pastors, you need to make the church love on the staff. Talk about what the staff does from the stage and let the church know when there are staff birthdays. You better push the church to show them love and honor. They will if you make it a value.

And hey, all you other ministry leaders, you better encourage that church to love on the pastor and his family. I mean really. That's how you change culture in an organization and even in a church. You impose an environment on them until it becomes normal, natural and accepted.

Leaders, we need to start looking for real gifted people to work in our churches; get them at an early age and make your offices fun and creative. Yes, yes, yes. I know character matters, too. But you can teach and mentor character. Gifts are installed by God at birth, so maybe think about that. For some of our churches perhaps the giving cycle has become an issue. Think about doing some business within the church with volunteers to bring in more money so your reach can improve. It's legal, and the IRS will show you how to do it properly and comply with every law.

I lead a church outside of Denver just up into the mountains. In 15 minutes, I can be down the mountain and into civilization; but up here, it seems like another country. Our community is pretty small (around 9,000 people currently), and so it isn't likely that we will build a 10,000 person mega church. Right now, we get about 800 on an average Sunday, 1,200 to 1,400 on Christmas Eve and Easter, and in the summer it drops to like four people. What can I say? It's Colorado.

We live where everyone vacations, so my church goes camping every weekend in the summer. That decrease in offering can kill a church's growth and mission. But we have several businesses, and some that are very profitable. We run a publishing company, a graphics/ marketing and printing business. We have a burger joint called The Angry Llama, a small country store, a state certified driving school, a T-shirt silk screening business and several others. Our businesses' incomes now has passed the church giving, and please know we have very generous people.

It's helped us buy 50 acres and fund the building of a recreation center we're planning. Now when we have budget short falls, we have many ways of making it work. We can afford a much bigger staff than most churches our size. We are able to employ 30 teen-agers, giving them meaningful opportunities to earn as they learn different trades.

Making money ourselves is how we have made the money serve us instead of bowing to wherever it comes from. Our leaders can make real decisions without worrying about who might leave and how much money we might be set back. Essentially, the leaders in the church all run the businesses so they are really the biggest donors. Intimidation and threats would just bounce off them. A funny thing happens when church leaders have their own ways of bringing in money; they have the ability to really lead and bring people to a powerful vision without having to be political. We decide we are going to do what God told us to do, and if we have to pay for it ourselves, we will. I personally get tired of pastors and ministry leaders whining about how if they just had more money, then they could really get on with their calling. Do you realize the phrase "Where God guides, He provides" is not an actual scripture? It's just a nice thought. The Bible teaches more along the lines of "Where God guides, we gotta go." And that may mean you have to find innovative ways to get your church off the ground. If companies can start in their basements and grow to become billion dollar corporations, then maybe we should stop playing the victims and grow up. Perhaps we should stop begging for the scraps from the marketplace table and go find our own place. I bet we would attract back some of the gifted ones who left when they see us taking on the resource challenge in cool ways. So giving is down in churches; that doesn't have to stop us.

Most of the way we do church has really been birthed out of the pain many leaders consistently carry. More than a few times our whole staff reconsidered staying in this profession. I can remember one of my lowest points was opening the door one morning and seeing several boxes left with a note. A family had gone school shopping for the coming school year, and they wanted to give some of their old clothes to us for our kids. Now look, I love hand-me-downs and promote sharing, but when I opened the box I didn't see clothes. I saw trash. One shoe was completely duct taped together. There was a small bag of socks that had no matches and another bag with seven gloves. Seven and only two that matched.

I realized at that moment how my family was thought of by these people. We were the leftovers. We should just be lucky to get their trash. I never wanted my staff, family or myself to feel that again. So we grew up and have become some of the strongest, most amazing people to serve with. The people who attend our church now ask how we are doing and then demand real answers. They are loving and strong. No one gets hurt because the easily-offended Christians get offended easily, and the controlling Christians realize there is no way to get hold of the steering wheel. The only ones who stayed are loving, fun, non-religious people who work hard and play harder.

Really, sometimes I feel like I'm the ministry of Willy Wonka, living in some magical land. But we all know magic isn't real, otherwise David Copperfield would have used it to stay famous. No, it's not magic; it's what happens when Christian leaders feel loved by their church.

We have an army of volunteers who help run, manage and account for them. It also doesn't distract from our mission as a church because we are always interacting with people in our businesses, and the fact that we are a church is unique to them. It opens doors that lead to the greatest relationships ever. But the thing I love most about doing these businesses is that we have become part of the everyday community with thousands of people. Just because someone may never come to your church doesn't mean you can't enjoy loving them on a different level.

Our church members have really let us be authentic people even though we are the leaders. That is why I'm free to say all the things in this chapter without worrying some may get mad and leave. We have already talked all this through together, because our congregation has chosen to love us which gives us, her leaders, the courage to try things not normally attempted in church. When churches love their leaders, it really frees them to try harder, risk and be creative. We are all allowed to say what movies we like, disagree on politics and even listen to great music of our choice without being looked down on. Our kids all feel very loved and included because people in the church make it a point to insert themselves into our lives in a real way. Every one of our senior staff has been offered jobs in other ministries around the country. They could have made a lot more money and had much more notoriety. We have all laughed them away. You see, our church loves us so much, my guess is the only way we are leaving will be in some sort of box. I have become convinced that love is the single most powerful force imaginable. When love is released and promoted in our churches, it will put an end to the church fight club mentality and make us all stand together as one. After that, only God knows what He will do with a bunch of misfits who choose to love each other. Possibly change the world? I'll keep you posted.

CHURCH
FIGHT
CLUB

Appetizers

According to New York Times

August 1, 2010

- 1,500 pastors leave their ministries each month due to burnout, abuse, or moral failure.
- 94% feel under pressure to have a perfect family.
- 90% work more than 50 hours a week.
- 70% of pastors don't have any close friends.

Of all the chances you can take in life,
one of the safest is to
give fallen people a second one.
#WhyWeEatOurOwn

#why we eat our own 9

And Now . . . a Brief Message From Ironman

"There goes my hero,
Watch him as he goes,
There goes my hero,
He's ordinary"
Foo Fighters - My Hero

In a touching and unexpected moment, actor Robert Downey Jr. defended, helped, and restored fellow actor and friend, Mel Gibson. Mel has had his share of issues that led most in the Hollywood industry to block him and refuse him any kind of meeting. Robert not only decided to get Mel back on his feet, but he did so publicly on a televised award show. With humility, he sacrificially confessed his own struggle with controlled substances; with tenderness (out of genuine forgiveness and friendship) and with hope, he said:

"I would ask that you join me, unless you are completely without sin (in which case you picked the wrong [expletive] industry) in forgiving my friend his trespasses and offering him the same clean slate you have me. Allowing him to continue his great and ongoing contribution to our collective art without shame. He's hugged the cactus long enough."

Ironman actually explained that it was Mel who had picked him up at his lowest moment, and helped restore him to a successful career again. And guess what? Mel returned to work. Hollywood can forgive and restore its failures.

NFL quarterback, Michael Vick admitted to conduct that was "not only illegal, but also cruel and reprehensible," according to the NFL commissioner. Vick served time for federal charges of animal abuse and gambling and was suspended indefinitely without pay. Yet Vick is the main character of one of the greatest comeback stories ever told. His rehabbed image is proof that when you say sorry, sincerely and remorsefully, for past transgressions - redemption is often on the way.

Andy Reid was the coach for the Philadelphia Eagles and decided to take the heat for bringing Vick in and giving him another chance. While other teams didn't want the bad press, the Eagles endured some real hell from various sources, including a lot of their fans. But today, Michael Vick is staying the course. He took the second chance given to him and is doing his best with it. The anger has died down considerably now, and all that is really left is a man doing what he was born to do. The NFL can forgive and restore people.

Martha Stewart, Kobe Bryant, Tiger Woods, Bill Clinton, and Charlie Sheen all had giant failures and PR nightmares; but yet, here they all are, doing okay and outliving their worst moments.

Why is it that America is so forgiving, and all the while the American Church is so unforgiving? While you think about that for a second, allow me to meet an argument that some may be thinking of now: "Well, we Christians are held to a higher standard than the world, so that's not the same." Okay, then please explain why Peter got restored by Jesus after he totally denied even knowing Him? I could cite several other moments in Scripture when people sinned or failed in their calling, and God still used them. But why? Explain why God used Peter after such a massive failure. Don't worry, I'll wait.

It can't be done. Not in any real intelligent or convincing way. But we, as the body of Christ, are doing this to each other way too often. It doesn't matter about the nature of your sin or the role you may have in the church; you could be targeted. We can hold every dark act or mistake against you and never let you out of jail for divorce, moral failure, bankruptcy, or drunk driving. It doesn't matter if you are the pastor or if you sit in the back pews. The American Christian Church may be the biggest prison system in the entire world. Only we don't cut people off from their freedoms; we just amputate their spirits. So to borrow a great line from the movie *Scent of a Woman*, "And there is no prosthetic for an amputated spirit."

I'm not going to propose I'm a great authority on our society, but let's face it, the world is far better at redeeming the fallen than the Church is. I don't know about you, but that fact doesn't taste good when I choke it down. Maybe we just don't like messiness.

Sin is always messy; that's why we call it sin. Maybe Christians have spiritual OCD. In fact, though most Christians understand sin is inevitable, we still despise it . . . unless, I do it. Then it's just a mistake, that's all. Perhaps we just hate pain. According to *ABC News*, 80 percent of all the prescription painkillers in the world are taken by Americans. What is hurting us so badly? Maybe we eat our own because we want to destroy all evidence that someone did something that brought us pain.

There was a trend in the 50s in which pregnant

teens just conveniently went away to have their babies. Well, that was one way of avoiding the problems associated with this taboo. The Church does this with the fallen, sometimes sending people away or hiding them. And sometimes we sacrifice them. Rarely do we allow our wounded to publicly apologize as society does. This is clearly because other people's sin exposes our own. We see ourselves in them. So, we deflect instead of empathize or openly relate.

But I think it's just that we don't know how to look at people through the eyes of our God. Rather, we have a nasty way of looking at people as if we ARE God. We are going to either be an advocate or an accuser. It's time every Christian pick a side. When people say "sorry," we all need to shift out of neutral and either forgive and restore, or we are going to have to own the fact that we will accuse and consume our wounded. We have examples for both in the Bible. Revelation reads that Satan stands before God, and he is the accuser of the brethren. The other example is in 1 John and reads that Jesus stands up for us as our advocate. We now, officially, have two examples to look to.

This is EVERY Christian's duty. No longer can we blame the church leaders for what is done. If Christians tolerate it then why change anything? When the people in the church start demanding grace and mercy for everyone, then its leaders will have to hear them. It will be like a revolution. In the end, living up to the standard Jesus set, is just too much for us. Okay then, how about Ironman?

According to the Mayo Clinic staff, the health benefits for forgiving others are:

-Healthier relationships

-Lower blood pressure

-Fewer symptoms of depression

-Lower risk of alcohol and substance abuse

-Less anxiety, stress and hostility

Appetizers

No one gets through life without being damaged.
Many die, but some choose to play damaged.
They are the heros.

#WhyWeEatOurOwn

#why we eat our own 10

Bridges . . . We're Doing It Wrong

"When I was a kid,
my grandfather was a preacher
He talked about God, yeah,
he was something like a teacher
He said God only helps those,
who learn to help themselves
He was a million miles from a million dollars
But you can never spend his wealth"
OneRepublic - Preacher

If you ever get the chance, you should watch a documentary called *The Bridge*. These filmmakers actually put cameras on the Golden Gate Bridge for one year to record one of the most heartbreaking things you will ever witness. During that year, they recorded over twenty people using that bridge to commit suicide. The Golden Gate Bridge is actually the second most common spot for suicide in the world, second only to a bridge in China. Since the bridge was built in 1937, there is no accurate number on how many have actually killed themselves from there, mostly because so many were never seen jumping and bodies get washed out to sea.

Of the numbers that are known, it is in the thousands. I'll admit that this film wrecked me. To this day, I cannot see a picture of the bridge without the image of people climbing over the rail, standing there for a few minutes, and then letting go. During the film, they actually try to understand some of these people and what led them there. In every case, you could factor in the one word. Hopeless.

It's true that man cannot live without hope. When a person has lost all hope, then perhaps ending one's life, instead of enduring miserable circumstances, is an option that may give them some type of twisted hope. And just like any living thing, the church in America has got to feel hope that things can get better, or it will continue to subconsciously do the things that are actually killing it. That goes for the Christians who have walked away from the Church saying, we aren't part of it. You may not attend one right now, but you are still part of Christ's church. So before we burn a bridge, we need to decide if we are willing to live on that side of the river forever. No, how we treat each other is every Christian's problem and so every one of us can help to fix it.

But what to do? Where can we start? I know for me that when I have seen the most change in my character and behavior, I have had to focus on the positive actions I needed to take and try to avoid the negative actions. For example: If I want to stop gossiping, then I don't just try to bite my lip and to avoid saying anything negative. Instead, everyday I try to say as many positive things about people as I can. It's hard to slip back into negative behavior when I'm consumed at working to say so much good.

If I want to forgive, then I can't simply sit around and fight my emotions of resentment. Instead, I force myself to see some type of value and good in the people who have treated me badly. When I do that long enough, the bad memories begin to be replaced again with ones of love and trust.

So let's get a punch list together of practices we can apply everyday, in a real way. If we change ourselves, we will impact change in others around us. In turn, when scores of us change, we actually begin to change our world.

First, if we have been wounded by another Christian, a church, a pastor, a church leader, or anyone at all, we need to forgive them. I know it's not fun, and it doesn't mean you have to go back to their particular church or back into their world. They may not even care that they hurt you, but this is about you getting free to be the person God needs you to be. If we carry bitterness, then the cycle of judgments, hate, and wounds will be carried on through us. Let the cycle end with us.

Okay, next let's go to the source for all things good and healthy in our relating pattern. 1 Corinthians 13, in my opinion, is the sum of all wisdom when it comes to making any life great or making any relationship work. In it, we are told about how love is the single greatest power on earth. The chapter actually takes a few shots at what Christians tend to believe is a bigger deal than love.

Spiritual gifts, prophecy, knowledge, faith that can move mountains, generosity, and even dying for our faith all get thrown under the bus together, if they are not done with love. The Scripture is telling us, in no uncertain terms, that love is the highest principle and activity we Christians can engage in. So it would really help if we all got on the same page as to what love really is.

You want to do an interesting experiment to see how far apart we are in our understanding of just basic things?

Think of a chair. Write it down on paper and put it in your pocket. Now throughout the day, ask at least 10 people you know to think of a chair and to describe it to you. Make notes on your paper about each one. At the end of the day, you will have a list with every kind of chair. Some will be chairs at their office, others will be a recliner in their living room, or perhaps a barstool from a local pub.

Now a chair is a pretty common thing, but depending on the need, it might not be a good fit. If you have ever watched an entire football game on a stool in a sports bar, you know why sitting in a recliner is much more fitting. So if we think so differently on something as simple as a chair, what makes us think that we are all on the same page when God tells us to love?

1 Corinthians 13 cuts all the confusion and mystery out, and gives us some actions we can inject into our lives to become more loving people. Here, let me share a few.

Love is patient. When we love people, we will not force them to move at our pace or even leave them behind. I remember when we brought our first child home. We enjoyed watching her begin to see the world around her. Over the years, she has grown and her mother and I have enjoyed every stage just as much - like when she learned to point, talk, stand, walk, ride a bike, and even drive. Although, the driving one has had its moments.

Because we love her, we have been completely fine with her pace in developing as a person. When she developed some different ways of looking at the world than I have, I enjoyed debating with her and watching her hold her own. She's fixing to leave for college soon, and I'm so excited about how much she is going to grow these next few years in that particular stage in her life. I'm not a fan of paying the bills, but she will never know that because I will do it gladly.

And no, odds are she won't read this, at least, not for a few years. I asked her when she thought she might read some of my books and was informed that when I added in a vampire love story or fighting werewolves, only then would she give it a go. As much as I tried to meet her request, the chapter I had entitled *Team Edward, Team Jacob, Team Jesus* never really tested well. You see, when you love someone, you don't mind doing life together at their pace.

Another attribute I enjoy is that love keeps no record of wrongs. I guess that's why I'm a big advocate for people getting second and third chances after they have failed. Maybe it's because it's built into our human spirit. When I see stories of soldiers returning home with missing arms and legs but determined to do what they love again, I am always moved.

Recently, I read about a guy who used to love rock climbing but had since lost his legs. His friends all helped design special equipment, and he began to learn how to climb again, just doing it a different way. He said he felt alive again. Yes! Love can cover mistakes and sin. Love teaches us to not live in those dark moments of our life any longer. To hold a person back from what they long to do because of a past failure, you hold a record of their wrong against them. And that's just not love. Love is a master set of keys that unlocks the prisons of guilt and shame we put ourselves in.

And possibly my favorite is: "Love always perseveres." Love can play with pain. One very powerful truth I try to impart to my kids, staff, friends, and the pastors I work with is something you can only learn from pain. The truth is that if you ever want to be great at anything, then at different times in your life, you are going to have to do whatever it is you do, hurt. True love will take hits but keeps coming day after day. Sure, you will get hurt, but that doesn't mean you're injured.

Every year, I coach my youngest son' s little league

football team. When I started doing this, he was just in the fourth grade, and we got all the kids that had never played before. The first few games took forever to finish because every other play, I had to go out on the field and pick up little crying boys who thought that they were dying. After a while, we started teaching them the difference between being injured and hurt. If your leg or arm won't move at all or is bent in ways you have never seen, then you're injured. Don't move.

However, if you can still move your arm or leg, it's just hurt. Try to get up and walk around a little. Maybe that sounds old school but "walk it off" does work. And you know what? These little guys got it! They would get up crying, angry, and scared . . . but they got up. And when a person gets up, it's the first step to healing.

I think it's fair to say that there are enough actions we can get from 1 Corinthians 13 to keep us busy and focused for a while. Truth is, we will all need to keep growing in love for the rest of our lives. And to be sure, everyone's hourglass is running. You have less time today than you did yesterday. And don't kid yourself, one day the last bit of sand will slip through, then that's a wrap!

I don't think about death as much as I used to when I was really sick, but I was recently reminded that understanding our own mortality can really change our priorities. It actually happened at the Denver Comic Con.

I'm not sure if any of you know what Comic Con is, but it is a convention of epic proportions for the super nerds and geeks. I had never been before, but after going, I doubt I'll ever miss one when they are held in Denver. I had paid a lot of money to go to a meet and greet with William Shatner. You know, Captain James T. Kirk from *Star Trek*.

I went for several reasons that kind of converged all at once. I am, of course, a big fan of *Star Trek* and, in my opinion, he was the first and best captain of the many that held that role. If you disagree, you are wrong on so many levels I couldn't unpack them here. But because this is a book about total honesty, I would like to let you know that I am available to talk to you directly in order to fix such a poor life decision.

But anyway, back to my reasons for going. One of the reasons is actually kind of sad. See, I grew up as a stepson and never really knew my real father. I met him a few times but he never really showed any interest in my life. My stepdad had his own kids, and you could easily see that they were a joy and I was kind of a duty. I wasn't abused, but I was just there. So with a void in my life and needing a father, I turned to men on TV to be my father. It actually had more of an effect on me than I could have ever known.

A few years ago, when I found out Tom Bosley, the dad from *Happy Days* died, I actual felt like crying. He was a dad and counselor to that whole gang, and so I kind of lived vicariously through them. There were a few other actors that I would say had an impact on me and they have all passed away. In fact, William Shatner was the only one left.

SO, when I heard he was in town and that if you paid enough, you could hang out with him for an hour, something really weird happened. I felt like it would be the closest I would ever get to experiencing a father/ son moment. Look, I know how stupid this sounds but it is what I felt. When the day arrived, I took one of my friends and staff member, Josh, with me to meet Bill. It was worth every cent. For over an hour, we sat around a little room with a handful of people and the captain.

Now, in his eighties, he is still sharp as a tack and funny to the core. But towards the end, I asked him what he felt his thoughts were at this time in his life.

He said he thought of dying a lot - he said not like he is afraid because he is still very healthy, but rather what he is going to miss. He said that he used to read about some new invention that was coming and thought it would be great, but he explained that when you get to this age, you realize you're going to hear about things that you may never see. He said he also thinks about those he loves and leaving more behind for them while he can. He then said something that made me feel like a kid being told something by a dad. "Soak it all up now guys, 'cause it goes fast. Be the best you can today."

It was such a powerful reminder from someone in the last part of his life. I don't want to leave anything in the tank. I want to live until I die. I want to be advanced at love and I really want to bring joy and laughter into the world, even if it's after I'm gone. I have given my wife very clear instructions as to what to write on my headstone. She, however, is not a fan of it (so we argue) but I'll win. My argument is that it's mine and I want to be fun.

It would, of course, have my name and then where it says my birth date, that's where things get fun. Here. Imagine seeing this at a cemetery. "Born: April 17th, 1972 – Died: In your arms tonight, must have been something you said." How can anyone not like the 80s reference? It will make people laugh, and laughter brings us hope, a hope that the Bible says, does not disappoint (Romans 5:5).

I, for one, don't want to look at Christianity one day like I look at the Golden Gate Bridge. I want to feel hope about the Church for my whole life. I want to try harder now and not simply blame others. I will be different, I will care, I will be responsible, and I will lighten up.

Maybe if we enjoyed our lives a little more, played a little more, laughed a lot more, we would be altogether better Christ-followers, and we would run our race to win again. And winners usually forget there is a race. They just love to run.

Michael Cheshire

In the end, all our lives will be
a dash between two dates on a
stone somewhere.
Make your dash count.
#WhyWeEatOurOwn

MICHAEL CHESHIRE
Author of *Why We Eat Our Own*

You can cite the usual biographical information about Michael Cheshire (born in Austin, Texas; became a born-again Christian at age 18; has been married for 18 years and has three children; served as a youth pastor), but it is really impossible to talk about Michael without describing his belief in the power of grace, his love of the lost, and his philosophies about how to reach them.

In 2008, Michael, his wife, Amy, and a group of friends started The Journey Church in the town of Conifer, Colorado, which had been nicknamed "the church graveyard." Journey now regularly attracts 800 people from the small, wooded community and has become a vibrant, growing, and integral part of this town of 9,000 residents.

Michael believes that churches grow when they can gain proximity to people. He believes that any venture that gets church people to interact with the public increases chances of developing a friendship, and friendship with Christ-followers can lead to friendship with Christ Himself.

As a pastor with an entrepreneurial spirit Michael

has found creative and unusual ways for the church to interact with the public. The church operates a state-approved driving school with the youth pastors serving as instructors. It also runs a full-service diner—The Angry Llama—staffed by church volunteers who wear T-shirts saying "The Church has left the building." Journey has a traditional publishing and marketing company and even a racecar. Not only do these ventures help church members rub shoulders with the community, but they have also funded a paid staff of 24 full-time and 12 part-time employees. The church was also able to buy 50 acres of land and will soon break ground for a recreation center that will host three gyms, a bowling alley, a theater, and a food court. Michael says it will be the place for the families of Conifer to come, since the community currently doesn't offer any such facilities.

Michael is the author of *How to Knock Over a 7-Eleven and Other Ministry Training*. He is a regular contributor to Leadership Journal and provides church consulting. He is also one of the Roundtable speakers—an invitation-only think tank of pastors and seminary teachers—that develop ideas on how to be an authentic New Testament church based on true grace and forgiveness.

RANSOM
Notes

BECAUSE WE ARE ALL
HELD HOSTAGE BY
SOMEONE WE LOVE.

MICHAEL AND AMY CHESHIRE

Coming Soon

A conference for churches that are about getting out of the box...and into everyone else's.
TrojanHorseCollective.com

For more info or to buy other books from Michael Cheshire visit him online at:

MichaelCheshire.com
Facebook.com/JourneyMike
Twitter.com/JourneyMike

ISBN: 978-0-9853811-3
FirstPunchPress.com
©First Punch Press 2013

Coming soon from
Jonathan Brozozog
and First Punch Press
WorthlessGrace.com

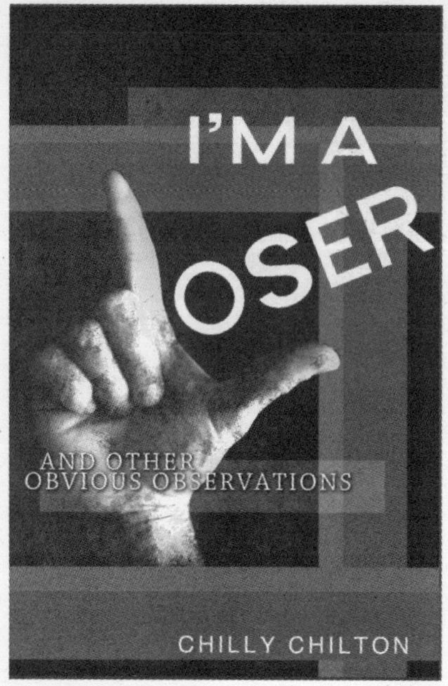
I'M A
OSER
AND OTHER
OBVIOUS OBSERVATIONS
CHILLY CHILTON

DRAEMON
STEVE
STARRETT

Look for these and other titles coming soon from First Punch Press.com!

Get your own
Church Fight Club Shirt
and other apparel @
FirstPunchPress.com